INSIGHTS

INSIGHTS

REFLECTIONS FROM 101 OF YALE'S MOST SUCCESSFUL ENTREPRENEURS

CHRIS LOPRESTI

MERRY DISSONANCE PRESS   CASTLE ROCK, COLORADO

Insights:
Reflections from 101 of Yale's Most Successful Entrepreneurs

Published by Merry Dissonance Press, LLC
Castle Rock, CO

FIRST EDITION
2015

Library of Congress Control Number: 2015910471
LoPresti, Chris, Author
Insights: Reflections from 101 of Yale's Most Successful Entrepreneurs
Chris LoPresti

ISBN 978-1-939919-23-6
1. Business & Economics
2. Entrepreneurship
3. Careers/General

Book Design and Cover Design © 2015
Cover Design by Victoria Wolf
Illustrations by Zach Harris
Book Design by Andrea Costantine
Editing by Donna Mazzitelli

For my parents,
Michael and Bonnie LoPresti,
who taught me to only start something
worth finishing and to pay it forward.
I love you both and owe you everything.

CONTENTS

Foreword   15

Preface   18

GETTING STARTED

Risk. *Brad Hargreaves*   25
Unshakable Conviction. *Chris Kincade*   27
The Value of Sweat Equity. *David S. Rose*   28
Focus on What Really Matters. *Chad Troutwine*   31
How to Hack Yale. *David Teten*   33
Riding the Roller Coaster. *Jesse D. Johnson*   35
Make It Fun. *Jordan Silbert*   37
Just Do It. *Elli Sharef*   38
Beating Up Your Idea. *Eric Meizlish*   40

STARTUPS

What Is A Startup? *Eric Ries*   44
Startups Require Passion. *Michael Ma*   49
Preparing to Do a Startup. *Ning Liang*   51
The Nine Key Elements of Hands-On Startup Creation.
    John R. Frank   52
Advice for Seed Stage Tech Startups. *Michael Seibel*   57
Have Passion and Be Meticulous. *William (Bill) D. Evers*   59
Fundamental Self-Confidence. *Paul Gu*   61
The Value of Preparation. *Roger McNamee*   65
Making an Adventure of Your New Venture.
    Peter S. H. Grubstein   67
Outlook. *Miles Lasater*   69

BECOMING AN ENTREPRENEUR

Advice from a Professor to Young Entrepreneurs.
  Barry Nalebuff   73
Is Entrepreneurship for You? Fritz Lanman   76
The Basics. Kathy Moskal   77
A To-Do List for the Aspiring Entrepreneur. Casey Gerald   79
An Entrepreneur's Luck. Donna Dubinsky   84
Can Entrepreneurs Actually Be Advised? Jeffrey Brenzel 87
The Entrepreneurial Life. Mark Gerson   89
Growing Out of Your Comfort Zone. Victor Cheng   93
Trust—The Way to Overcome Uncertainty. Patricia Brett   95
The Case for Humility. Justin Borgman   99
An Entrepreneurial Checklist. Tobin Fisher   101
Jump at Opportunity. Sander Daniels   105
Entrepreneur Your Life. Gregg Vanourek   107

MOTIVES AND MOTIVATION

Are Entrepreneurs Really the Happiest People on Earth?
  Jane Park   112
Nothing Else. Patrick Foley, Ph.D.   115
It Gives Me a Headache. Steve Gottlieb   117
Doing Well and Doing Good. Jens Molbak   125
Watch the Parking Meters. Steve Tomlin   128
Difference Between Business Development and Sales.
  Victor Wong   131
Sink or Swim. Julia Pimsleur   135
Connect Your Passion to Helping Others. Marc A. Perry   137
A Dose of Pragmatism. Sheldon Gilbert   139
Work with What and Who You Love.
  Tom Lehman and Ilan Zechory   142
Hate to Be Him. Rob Long   145
Fall in Love with a Problem. Sandeep Ayyappan   148
Passion Above All. Kevin Lee   153

PEOPLE

It Really Is the People. *David Meyers, Ph.D.*   158

Yes. Your People Is the Secret. *Ingrid Stabb*   160

Pick Your Co-Founders Wisely. *Alexandra Cavoulacos*   163

Like Good Friends. *J.B. Schramm*   165

Be Shameless—But Genuine—About Networking.
  Jonathan Swanson   167

Wisdom Based on Experience. *Peter O. Crisp*   169

Finding Your Team. *Eugene A. Ludwig*   170

Your Team Is Your Best Asset. *Brynne Herbert*   172

The Key to Hiring. *Kevin Ryan*   173

It's Still About the People. *Bob Casey*   175

Two Seconds. *Mara Segal*   179

Let Your Customers Teach You. *Anna Barber*   181

BEING THE BEST

Accomplish Something Every Day. *Richard Thalheimer*   187

Three Essentials to a Company's Success. *Lauren Monahan*   189

A Venture Culture. *Robert S. Adelson*   191

Intuition vs. Emotion. *Ben Jacobs*   195

Constant Striving. *Rohini B. Shah*   197

You Must Love LaMarcus Thompson. *Winston Bao Lord*   199

Execution is Everything. *Scott C. Johnston*   201

Gifting. *Dave Lieberman*   203

Living the 80/20 Rule. *Mike Del Ponte*   205

The Perfection of Imperfection. *Mie-Yun Lee*   206

What All Entrepreneurs Share. *Jessica Jewell Ogilvie*   208

The Value We Each Bring. *Louise Langheier*   210

So Many Stones. *Jordan Goldberg*   212

THE PATH IS NOT ALWAYS STRAIGHT

Why Work Is a Four-Letter Word. *Chris DeVore*   217

Moving the Needle. *Kevin J. Delaney*   220

Learning Through Experience. *Lise Laurin*   223

Making Decisions. *Rick Field*   225

Follow the Old Soldier. *Alex Selkirk*   228

Kissing the Stanley Cup. *Bing Gordon*   233

PERSEVERANCE

There Is A Way! *Mark T. Volchek*   238

On Failure. *Matthew O. Brimer*   239

How to Reach Your Destination. *Noah Glass*   241

A Team of One. *Scott Kaylie*   243

Keep Trying. *Al Zuckerman*   245

"No" Doesn't Mean "No"—It Just Means "Not Right Now!"
   Jennifer Carter Fleiss   246

Don't Give Up. *Linda Tong*   249

Unplug. *Pete Land*   251

The Chicken Itch. *Marc Cenedella*   252

FROM EXPERIENCE

Two Pieces of Advice. *Willis "Chip" Arndt, Jr.*   261

Ten Things I Wish I Had Known Before Founding a Company.
   Kate L. Harrison   264

Four Lessons They Don't Teach in Business School.
   Seth Goldman   270

Optimize. *Dan Friedman*   275

You Are Always a Shoeshiner. *Lee Mergy*   273

Three Things I Wish I'd Learned Earlier. *Linda Rottenberg*   287

Hard-Won Lessons from the Bottom of Silicon Valley.
   Scott Faber   279

Avoiding Pitfalls. *Frederick W. Smith*   281

The Top Ten Avoidable Mistakes of Entrepreneurs.
  William H. Draper III   *289*
Passion. Persistence. and Pragmatism. *Sanjay H. Patel*   *292*
Words to the Wise. *Jon Carson*   *295*
Jump. *Damon Danielson*   *297*
It's Not All About You. *Mitch Kapor*   *299*
Be Amazing. *Markus Moberg*   *301*
I Wish Someone Had Told Me. *Cornelius McNab*   *305*

Acknowledgments   306

About the Author   309

Elis Inc. and Proceeds   310

Let's Stay Connected   311

About the Press   312

Foreword.

Sean Glass
Founder, Yale Entrepreneurial Society
Founder, Higher One Holdings
Founder and Managing General Partner, Acceleprise. VC
Founder and CEO, Advantia Health

IT HAD BEEN A LONG NIGHT AT THE ZOO, AND I WAS not ready for an inquisition by the infamous Dean Betty T and Dean Brodhead. Of course, it was my fault, as I hadn't started the assignment until way too late in the week. The Zoo, as it's commonly known, is the computer cluster in Yale's computer science building. It's where aspiring CS majors aggregated, particularly when we were working through programming assignments. Seeing our submission fail a few unit tests as the sun rose over the graveyard opposite the building gave new meaning to the phrase "graveyard shift."

Betty Trachtenberg (or Betty T, as students tended to refer to her) was Yale's Dean of Students, and Dick Brodhead was the Dean of Yale College. I had been summoned, along with the two other co-founders of the Yale Entrepreneurial Society (YES), to a meeting with the two deans, who had cryptically said they wanted to understand what we were all about.

We were a little nervous about the meeting. When we founded YES, we had purposefully pushed the boundaries of what an undergraduate organization was supposed to be, because we didn't want to be *just* another undergraduate organization. We wanted to be the organization that knitted together all Yale entrepreneurs, be they students, alumni, faculty, or staff.

So what were we all about? Were we the "business guys" that liberal arts institutions viewed with skepticism, or were we something else?

Maybe it was the lack of sleep, but to me the answer was clear.

Entrepreneurship is about having an idea and then figuring out how to make it a reality. It's about a melding of knowledge, resources, and creativity to create something of value to the world. Too often, we think of entrepreneurship only as the act of building a large tech company or the starting of a small business. But that's not it. Deciding to write and publish a book or spinning up a new product within a larger company is also entrepreneurship.

When I enrolled at Yale, I wasn't quite sure what I wanted to be. It was 1998, and the media was starting to look forward to the millennium celebration. Many magazines published issues that summarized the previous 100 years. One magazine in particular caught my attention. It provided an overview of the 100 greatest builders of the last century. Suddenly I knew: that was it. That's what I wanted to do. I wanted to be a builder. I wanted to start and build companies, and my big hairy audacious goal was that I wanted to be in the 2098 issue of that magazine (okay, so magazines won't exist then, but the equivalent!). That idea led me to the founding of YES, Higher One (NYSE:ONE), and my founding of Acceleprise and Advantia Health.

The following day, when we were in that room with the two Yale deans, they asked us, "Why Yale? Why are we a place for entrepreneurs, and what does it take to succeed as an entrepreneur?"

I answered that to succeed as an entrepreneur takes hard work, luck, and the ability to understand a business from many angles. Additionally, a liberal arts education can be incredibly empowering in helping someone along the path to entrepreneurial success.

In the years since that meeting, my original explanation has been proven accurate, as I have had the privilege of meeting many successful Yale entrepreneurs. From the cotton gin to Pinterest, Yale grads have shown the ability to create value across many different industries and markets.

This book is an example of the power of the collective knowledge and wisdom of Yale's entrepreneurs and investors. You've probably heard a lot about Stanford, Harvard, or MIT when it comes to entrepreneurship. So why should you read a book written by Yale entrepreneurs? I think it's simple. The breadth of experience, ideas, and advice you will gain from this book is unlike any other collection I have seen. It helps to answer the question, better than I ever could, about why Yalies have had success founding companies, starting world-changing nonprofits, or creating venture capital powerhouses.

Being an entrepreneur is a noble, but difficult, endeavor. Whatever you are creating from scratch, I'm sure you will find something in this book that helps you achieve success, and for substantially less than the cost of Yale tuition! Enjoy, and boola boola!

Preface.

AS ALL ENTREPRENEURIAL ENDEAVORS BEGIN, THIS book started with an idea. In the spring of 2012, I graduated from Yale College, eager to determine my next steps in life. Earlier that year, I had started a rough shell of a company, developed a minimal viable product, acquired one paying customer, and was trying to decide if I was going to go all-in and attempt to turn it into a business or, like many of my classmates, take a more traditional job, with generous benefits and a guaranteed salary.

It occurred to me that the incredible Yale network, which was something the Office of Admissions had so dutifully highlighted to my parents and me four years earlier, offered plenty of experience to answer my specific questions. It seemed that it could only help me to consult with alums who had been in my situation. So I reached out to a handful of successful bulldogs who had started their own businesses and asked them for advice. The feedback I received was so helpful that I wanted to share it with future graduates of Yale and anyone wrestling with the challenges of turning an idea into a company.

The style of this book is a collection of easily-digestible advice from these successful entrepreneurs. The advice is grouped by topic, and the topics roughly ordered in the stages of creating a business, but many of the suggestions, hints, tips, tricks, and warnings span more than one topic. In order to get the most out of this book, I highly recommend that you first read the book in its entirety to get a feel for the many decisions and challenges you'll face on your path as an entrepreneur. I then recommend that you go back to each chapter as you move through that stage in your company's life to refresh your memory and to take in the advice through the acute lens of solving a specific problem or overcoming a specific obstacle. Two to three pieces of insight should make great bedtime reading—they're meatier than a Tweet and contain more useful information, but they're concise and focused enough for you to ruminate on a few key lessons at a time. Every one of these lessons has been learned the hard way by its author.

The contributors range widely in experience and background. At the time the advice was initially submitted, the youngest participant was one of Peter Thiel's 20 under 20, and the oldest contributor was William H. Draper III, one of the fathers of venture capital. While many successful technology entrepreneurs are included in this book, you will also find advice and insights from founders of Fortune 100 companies, retail and e-commerce powerhouses, syndicated chefs, bestselling authors, global nonprofits, media moguls, and early investors in companies such as Facebook, Yelp, Pinterest, Zynga, Apple, Cisco, Yahoo, and more.

Once you begin your journey down the rabbit hole of entrepreneurship, you'll quickly discover that time is your most precious resource. My goal for this book, and the desire of each of the participants, is that their experiences (successes and mistakes), will help you avoid pitfalls, make better choices, and use the time you save to make your company or organization even better. As one of the contributors writes, you should be shameless about borrowing. This library of advice has been assembled and classified for you to borrow as often as you need.

My personal experiences at Yale led me to appreciate the strong network of successful alumni the school has created over its more than 300-year history, but I know there are many other excellent universities with excellent networks of equally successful individuals. I hope these other schools (or any community out there) replicate this model for consolidating the best of their collective knowledge to build their community and help others execute on their innovative ideas.

Chris LoPresti
August 2015

GETTING STARTED.

making a
BET
on
YOURSELF

Risk.

Brad Hargreaves
Co-Founder, General Assembly

STARTING A BUSINESS IS RISKY. ON ANY GIVEN DAY, any number of things represents mortal threats to a young company. I was told this time and time again while I was starting my first business. But what I wasn't told was that while any individual venture is extremely risky, choosing entrepreneurship as a career path is comparatively safe. As an entrepreneur, you're making a bet on yourself.

Starting a business is risky. This is indisputable. The vast majority of businesses fail, and some take their owners down with them. But many of those entrepreneurs bounce back to do bigger and better things, buoyed by the knowledge and experience of a failed venture. That experience not only enables new entrepreneurial successes, but tends to be the kind of broad-based, life-altering understanding that opens up all kinds of unexpected doors personally and professionally. It's not uncommon for entrepreneurs to leverage the experience of a failed venture to pay the bills by consulting in that vertical with larger companies. For example, a friend who was forced to shut down his business in the social media space leveraged the expertise he'd gained building his business to land consulting gigs he never would've been able to get before. There's a reason you don't see failed entrepreneurs panhandling in the street despite the high startup failure rate.

Starting a business is risky. In the short term, we're all in grave danger from our own stupid decisions. But over time, with the benefits of experience and wisdom, our biggest threat is counterparty risk, or the grave danger of others' stupid decisions. And if the past decade has proven anything—from Enron to Lehman—it's that the stupidity and short-sightedness of others can be the most devastating threat of all. Large companies are complex organisms, and while the jeopardies they face are less obvious than those of startups, they exist nonetheless. From partner disputes blowing up law firms to department-wide layoffs to large-scale fraud and accounting malfeasance, the forty-year career and path to the gold watch isn't what it used to be.

Starting a business is risky. But the risk is clear and known from the start. And the risk is dependent on our own ability to make good decisions, plan appropriately, and find help when it's needed. At the end of the day, it's on us.

Unshakable Conviction.

Chris Kincade
CEO, 11 Picas Digital

BEFORE UNDERTAKING AN ENTREPRENEURIAL EF-
fort, here is my advice:

⇨ Read *The Art of War*. It's a bit cliché to tout Sun Tzu's treatise on military strategy as an entrepreneur's bible, but you are, in fact, undertaking a campaign, or rather a series of campaigns, that will require sensible planning, supreme adaptability, and audacious leadership. Assimilate these concepts.

⇨ Partner carefully and thoughtfully. Ideas are about execution. Understand the scope of your product, distribution, sales, marketing, business development, and finance needs. Then ensure you have expertise at every skill position.

⇨ Write and revise your business plan continuously. Writing well and clearly on your strategy is essential. Until your business reaches maturity, you should rearticulate the plan on a regular basis.

⇨ Build a plan and team that allow you to proceed with unshakable conviction. If you cannot parry adversity, your plan or team wasn't right.

The Value of Sweat Equity.

David S. Rose
Serial entrepreneur, angel investor, startup mentor
CEO, Gust; Founder, New York Angels
Managing Partner, Rose Tech Ventures

FIRST-TIME ENTREPRENEURS WHO ARE PUTTING TO-gether a startup team often try to figure out what the ratio of equity compensation should be for founders putting in sweat equity, compared to those putting in cash investments, or getting paid a regular salary. In fact, there is *no* specific ratio between "sweat equity" and cash in a venture. It's actually not a good way to think about the issue.

The bottom line is that cash is cash is cash ... and everything else is "not cash." The reason is that cash is fungible, which means it can be interchanged for everything else, from programming skills to vacations on the Riviera. Other things, such as one's particular time and effort, are not.

A better way to think about this is to separate two aspects of the "sweat" that one puts into a new venture. These are critically different and have very different economic attributes attached to them.

The first is the entrepreneurial value of the founder(s) in a new venture. This is what happens when someone starts an enterprise and creates something of value. So if you start a company and then raise a round of angel investment at, say, a $2,000,000 pre-money valuation, the entrepreneurial value of the time and effort it took you to get to that point is ... $2,000,000. The point is that the value created has absolutely nothing to do with a quantified effort that it took to get there. You might have created that value by slaving eighteen hours a day, seven days a week for five years (in which case the value of the sweat equity is $8.70 per hour), or you might have created that value by having a brilliant concept, execution plan, and team that you pulled together in two weeks of leisurely work (in which case the value of the sweat equity is $25,000 per hour).

The second component is the replacement cost of the specific skills and effort that are involved in the particular work. So if the same specific tasks could have been achieved by paying a programmer (or marketer or part-time CFO), say, $2,000 on a short-term contract, then that is *exactly* what the replacement cost value of the work would be.

In practice, once a company has been funded and a valuation established, "sweat equity" contributed after that point is usually compensated based *only* on the replacement cost number, either 1:1 (that is, the nominal salary, or what you would have been paid if the cash had been on hand) is simply accrued, or some other ratio (say, 25% or 50% extra), in recognition of the fact that you're willing to take the risk that you will never be paid if things don't work out.

FOCUS ON WHAT REALLY MATTERS

Focus On What Really Matters.

Chad Troutwine
Co-Founder, Veritas Prep
Producer of the film *Freakonomics*

DURING MY SECOND YEAR IN THE MBA PROGRAM AT Yale, I stood before a panel of judges at the largest student business plan competition in the world. After a year of planning one of my businesses, someone finally asked me the question I wish I had heard when I first started the process.

The previous year, I had won Yale's competition and recruited my best friend and classmate Markus Moberg (SOM '02) to partner with me at an event in New York City. One of the judges—serial entrepreneur and Green Mountain Coffee founder and CEO, Robert Stiller—asked me, "What's your exit strategy?" I deftly clicked to the PowerPoint slide that included boilerplate language about competitor acquisitions and public offerings. Before I had a chance to speak, he said, "No, I mean your *real* exit strategy." Without breaking eye contact I responded, "Markus and I want our children to run this business one day." Stiller smiled, jotted down some notes, and thanked us for our time. As a result of his question, I got the opportunity to see clearly what we wanted to achieve.

That night, our team won the competition, and I was selected as the Forbes Future Capitalist of the Year. Stiller knew this wasn't some casual, quick flip business idea. We were willing to pour everything we had into building a foundation that would last for decades. From that moment forward, there was no question what would happen next. Markus and I devoted every waking moment to our business and launched it one month after our graduation from the School of Management. We turned down all investment offers and built a pure bootstrap company with no debt and no venture capital.

Starting with one college intern, Veritas Prep is now home to approximately 720 instructors, admissions consultants, and education experts in more than 100 global cities. The number of students who prefer live online prep (as opposed to physical, in-person prep) has accelerated rapidly. We don't need as many instructors spread out all over the world because they can now reach students remotely. It's fascinating, really. We can now have one of the best instructors in the world teach in San Francisco from a live online studio and reach 50 students based all over the globe. That was rare three years ago and impossible ten years ago.

The market and the technology will change multiple times while building your company, so it's important to have the end goal in mind to keep you grounded and focused.

How to Hack Yale.

David Teten
Partner, ff Venture Capital
Founder, Harvard Business School Alumni Angels of Greater New York

HERE'S A BRIEF EXCERPT FROM A BOOK I'M WRITING, *Hack your Education: How to Squeeze Maximum Value from College or Graduate School.* You can see a webinar and a full draft of the book at teten.com/education.

Take the "obituary view." Write your obituary and see if you're happy with the impact you've "had" on the world. If your career and personal decisions don't enable you to achieve what's in your obituary, find options that enable you to have a bigger impact. Find what you love (enough to do it for free, if necessary), and then find a way to make a career in it (the old "make your hobby your career"). That said, consider the counsel of the book, *The Startup of You,* which correctly argues that you should consider your career entrepreneurially, looking opportunistically for pivots that will put you in a more advantageous position.

Think of your long-term goal (startup CEO, managing director at investment bank, full-time parent, etc.), and then identify the most common path that other people in that job have taken to achieve it. Most very successful people identify a career in which they are interested and for which they are well-suited, and then work very hard to advance up the relevant ladder for that career. As members of the Internet madness 1.0 generation (1998-2000) learned, the only real shortcut to success is pure luck. It is not wise to rely on pure luck to advance your career. To structure your thinking, there are basically three categories of jobs: working in companies, advising companies, and investing in companies. Choose one and excel.

If your goal includes effecting social change (e.g., promoting a certain social policy), then you need to choose the level at which you want to do so. There are four ways to effect change:

⇨ 1st Order: Founder. Includes entrepreneur, scientist, activist, organizer, elected politician. You do the hard work of building an organization.

⇨ 2nd Order: Investor. Important part of the ecosystem. You can make change happen by finding and funding the right Founders to effect change.

⇨ 3rd Order: Advisor. Includes consultants, lawyers, investment bankers. You consult to Founders. You rarely have equity.

⇨ 4th Order: Thought Leader: educators, media, authors, conference organizers. You can help to frame the discussion and spotlight certain people, but you have very little power to effect change directly. E.g., if you give a keynote or a front cover story to a great Founder doing work you think important, all you can do is hope that someone in the crowd will fund/support her. So your impact is highly indirect. No equity.

Riding the Roller Coaster.

Jesse D. Johnson
Founder, Q Collection
Founder, Telluride Venture Accelerator

STARTING AN ENTERPRISE (BE IT FOR- OR NOT-FOR-profit) is a roller coaster. You can't predict the great and disappointing turns that are to come. There are only two things that are certain. First, there will be a lot of both, and second, the ride is long.

It is important to celebrate the good turns but don't let them cloud your perspective. Similarly, during the bad turns, remember that they are inevitable and that they, too, will pass. If you let yourself fly too high during the highs or fall too low during the lows, you will be exhausted.

Building a great enterprise requires long-term commitment. Too many distractions—up or down—can take your eye off the end goal.

MAKE IT FUN

Make It Fun.

Jordan Silbert
Founder, Q Drinks

STARTING A BUSINESS WORTH STARTING IS INEVITA-
bly going to be a long hike, so you better find a way to enjoy it; in
fact, make having a good time a high priority for you and your team.

I've learned that one of the biggest risks you face as an entrepreneur is giving up because the struggle is not worth it—everything
is going to be harder and take longer than you expect when you're
starting out. But if you're willing to push on long enough, you will
usually win. So figure out a way to make it fun.

Just Do It.

Elli Sharef
Co-Founder, HireArt

THE PROMPT FOR THIS SUBMISSION WAS "ADVICE I wish I had gotten." Frankly, I'm glad I didn't have a lot of advice, or I might not have started this company. After reading all the posts about all the mistakes you can make (wrong co-founders, wrong idea, wrong time, wrong investors, wrong approach), you may think it's impossible to start a company. So here's my advice: Just go for it. Take the plunge. Don't overthink it. Just do it.

My biggest problem in the beginning was decision-fatigue: I thought every tiny decision mattered oh-so-much. And in truth, a lot of them really did matter. But worrying about them and over-thinking everything doesn't help. Make sure you are passionate and know a bit about your field. Pick a co-founder whom you trust and who is smart and ambitious. And then just start. The biggest reason entrepreneurs fail is because they never even start. So start.

When we started in YCombinator, here's how it went down:

⇨ We got to our first office hours and told Paul Graham (PG) we were "hoping to build our product over the next two months." He told us to go build it in a week and come back to show him.

⇨ We came back the week after with a fairly crappy version of our product. PG: "Okay, but how many clients are using it?" HireArt: "Umm, only one." PG: "Okay, go get fifteen new clients by next week and come back and tell me about them."

⇨ We came back the week after with fifteen clients. PG: "Okay, so how much revenue have you made?" HireArt: "Umm, we are giving it away for free right now." PG: "Okay, go make revenue over the next week and come tell us about it."

⇨ We came back the week after with a tiny bit of revenue. PG: "Okay, but why on earth haven't you launched???" HireArt: "Launched? Like publicly? We don't even really have a homepage yet." PG: "So go make a homepage tonight and launch next week."

⇨ We made a homepage within a few days and launched.

Nothing was perfect and I felt embarrassed and rushed at each step. It was uncomfortable because I thought products needed to look professional to be ready for launch. And then someone at YCombinator said, "If you're not embarrassed, you've waited too long to launch your product."

Aha! That's the key! It's *okay* for it to be less-than-perfect as long as the basic tool is good enough to give users a basic idea of what you're making.

It's that simple. YCombinator always told us to just push stuff out, make things happen, go fast. If I've got any advice, it's the same advice we got: Just do it. Make your product. Get people to use it. Launch. Don't overthink it. You'll make mistakes. If you're a good entrepreneur, you'll learn from them.

Beating Up Your Idea.

Eric Meizlish
Co-Founder and COO, Procured Health

THE DEDICATION AND PERSEVERANCE REQUIRED TO be a successful entrepreneur is hardly a secret. But I'd like to touch upon the stage before tears are shed and blood is spilled. Before you dive in headfirst. Before you make the biggest investment you've ever made, with the scarcest assets you have (your time and energy).

Take your idea—which you believe the world desperately needs, which you've spent countless hours dreaming about, sculpting in your mind, and molding into your masterpiece—and take two large steps back from it so that you are far enough away to see what it is and what you hope it will become. Now critique it. Really beat it up. Poke holes in it. Slash it to pieces. Ask the tough questions, specifically on two crucial dimensions: feasibility and payoff.

Feasibility: Why won't this work? Why will anybody care about your efforts, download your app, or pay for your service when there is a world of others out there? Why are you and your team the ones who will deliver? Why are you different? Ask yourself all the tough questions that an investor, who doesn't really want to invest anyway, will ask. Then convince him that he's wrong. If this isn't trivial, you may be dramatically underestimating the risk you are taking and overestimating your likelihood of success.

Payoff: Say you are successful at launching a real business—firstly, congratulations. Now what? Have you built something substantial and sustainable that will accrete value for your users and customers? Who is paying you their hard-earned cash, and are you delivering value that makes it worthwhile? Will your business continue to grow and improve, or will the pace of innovation plateau soon after launch? Is there a material risk that it will disappear as quickly as it arrived, as attention shifts to the next new thing? For how long will you be able to keep your customers, and why? Is your operation scalable? How do your economics evolve as the business grows? And is this an effort that you want to be dedicated to for the foreseeable future? How large is your reward, really?

Don't expect to be able to answer these questions by yourself. Go talk to people; however, not your family, friends, and prospective partners. Talk to those who will be your potential customers, who don't really care about your feelings. Ask them if they'll buy what you are selling. Ask them what other problems they have, and explore ways you might be able to solve those as well. Figure out what they are doing about those problems right now, what services they are using, who they are paying, and develop conviction about how you can do it differently and better. Take your time, be thorough, but always keep pushing forward. You'll know when you are ready to take the next step.

Then the real work begins.

STARTUPS.

What Is A Startup?

Eric Ries

Author, *The Lean Startup: How Today's Entrepreneurs Use Continuous Innovation to Create Radically Successful Businesses*

I THINK MOST PEOPLE HAVE A FAIRLY SPECIFIC IMAGE that gets conjured up when they hear the word startup. Maybe it's the "two guys in a garage" made famous by HP, or the idea of Jobs and Wozniak walking barefoot and shaggy through the Homebrew Computer Club. Maybe it's the more recent wunderkinds like Zuckerberg or Brin and Page. What all of these pictures have in common is a narrative that goes something like this: scrappy outsiders, possessed of a unique genius, took outrageous risks and worked incomprehensible hours to beat the odds.

But this cinematic view of entrepreneurs is flawed in many ways. Let's start with the most basic. It leads people to mistakenly believe that any time they see two guys in a garage attempting the impossible, that's a startup. Wrong. It also causes them to miss the numerous other kinds of startups that appear in less-glamorous settings: inside enterprises, nonprofits, and even governments. And because both small businesses and startups have a high mortality rate, sometimes these images lead us to believe that any small business is a startup. Wrong again.

So let's begin with a definition of a startup that captures its essential nature and tries to leave behind the specific associations of the most famous startups.

A startup is a human institution designed to deliver a new product or service under conditions of extreme uncertainty.

Let's take each of these pieces in turn. First, I want to emphasize the human institution aspect, because this is completely lost in the "two guys in a garage" story. The word "institution" connotes bureaucracy, process, even lethargy. How can that be part of a startup? Yet, the real stories of successful startups are full of activities that can rightly be called institution-building: hiring creative employees, coordinating their activities, and creating a company culture that delivers results. Although some startups may approach these activities in radical ways, they are nonetheless key ingredients in their success.

Isn't the word "human" redundant in this definition? What other kinds of institutions are there, anyway? And yet, we so often lose sight of the fact that startups are not their products, their technological breakthroughs, or even their data. Even for companies that essentially have only one product, the value the company creates is located not in the product itself but with the people and their organization that built it. To see proof of this, simply observe the results of the large majorities of corporate acquisitions of startups. In most cases, essential aspects of the startup are lost, even when the product, its brand, and even its employment contracts are preserved. A startup is greater than the sum of its parts; it is an acutely human enterprise.

And yet the newness of a startup's product or service is also a key part of the definition. This is a tricky part of the definition, too. I prefer to take the most expansive possible definition of product, one that encompasses any source of value for a set of people who voluntarily choose to become customers. This is equally true of a packaged good in a grocery store, an ecommerce website, a nonprofit social service, or a variety of government programs. In every case, the organization is dedicated to uncovering a new source of value for customers, and cares about the actual impact of its work on those customers (by contrast, a monopoly or true bureaucracy generally doesn't care and only seeks to perpetuate itself).

It's also important that we're talking innovation, but this should also be understood broadly. Even the most radical new inventions always build upon previous technology. Many startups don't innovate at all in the product dimension, but use other kinds of innovation: repurposing an existing technology for a new use, devising a new business model that unlocks value that was previously hidden, or even simply bringing a product or service to a new location or set of customers previously underserved. In all of these cases, innovation is at the heart of the company's success.

Because innovation is inherently risky, there may be outsized economic returns for startups that are able to harness the risk in a new way—but this is not an essential part of the startup character. The real question is: "What is the degree of innovation that this business proposes to accomplish?"

There is one last important part of this definition: the context in which the innovation happens. Most businesses—large and small alike—are typically excluded by this context. Startups are designed to confront situations of extreme uncertainty. To open up a new business that is an exact clone of an existing business—all the way down to the business model, pricing, target customer, and specific product—may, under many circumstances, be an attractive economic investment. But it is not a startup, because its success depends only on decent execution—so much so that this success can be modeled with high accuracy. This is why so many small businesses can be financed with simple bank loans; the level of risk and uncertainty is well enough understood that a reasonably intelligent loan officer can assess its prospects.

Thus, the land of startups is a unique place where the risks themselves are unknown. Contrast this with other high-risk situations, like buying a high-risk stock. Although the specific payoff of a specific risky stock is not known, investing in many such stocks can be modeled accurately. Thus, a decent financial advisor can give you a reasonably accurate long-term expected return for a set of risky stocks. When the "risk premium" is known, we are not in startup land. In fact, when viewed in retrospect, most startups appear like no-brainers. Probably the most famous example today is Google. How did we ever live without it? Building that particular product was not nearly as risky as it seemed at the time; in fact, I think it is a reasonable inference to say that it was almost guaranteed to succeed. It just wasn't possible for anyone to know that ahead of time.

Startups are designed for the situations that cannot be modeled, are not clear-cut, and where the risk is not necessarily large—it's just not yet known. I emphasize this point because it is necessary to motivate large amounts of the theory of the lean startup. Fundamentally, the lean startup is a methodology for coping with uncertainty and unknowns with agility, poise, and ruthless efficiency. It is a completely different experience from the equally hard job of executing in a traditional kind of business, and my goal is not to disparage those other practitioners—after all, most startups aspire to become non-startups someday.

Still, these differences matter, because the "best practices" that are learned in other contexts do not transplant well into the startup soil. In fact, the most spectacular startup failures result when people were in a startup situation but failed to recognize it, or failed to recognize what it meant for their behavior.

This definition is also important for what it excludes. Notice that it says nothing about the size of the company involved. Big companies often fail because they find themselves in a startup situation but are unable to reorient in time to cope with this situation; this specific pathology is explored in *The Innovator's Dilemma*. This kind of crisis can be precipitated by many external factors: macroeconomic changes, trade policy, technological change, or even cultural shifts. But most often, the entrant of a startup into a previously calm market precipitates this kind of crisis. This has significant implications for general managers in enterprise, about which you can read more in the article, "Is Entrepreneurship a Management Science?" at HBR.

Startups Require Passion.

Michael Ma
Founder, TalkBin.com

BECOMING AN ENTREPRENEUR ISN'T SOMETHING you become inspired by others to do; the drive to do a startup should come from within.

There really is no way to learn how to do a startup other than actually starting one. Your first startup will probably fail; it's what you do after you've found out you failed that really matters.

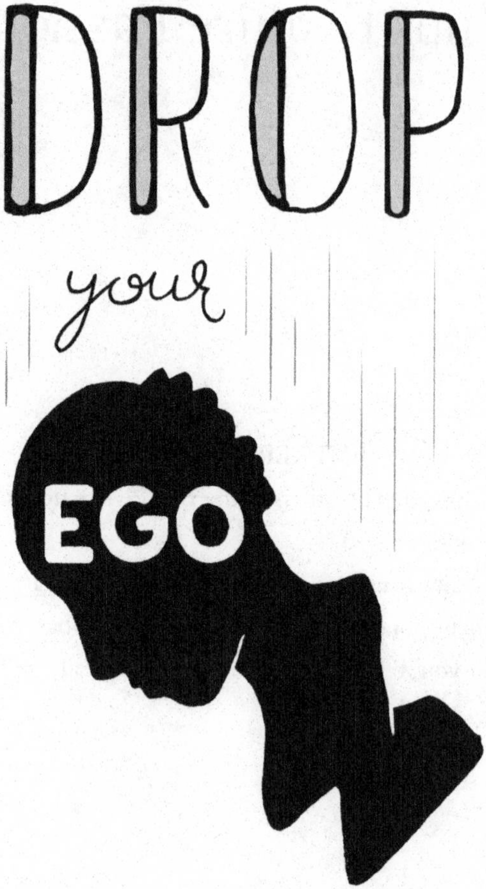
DROP
your
EGO

Preparing to Do a Startup.

Ning Liang
Co-Founder, HealthSherpa

CAREER ADVICE

Early on in your career, put yourself in situations where you are the dumbest guy in a room of experts or star performers. Then, drop your ego, work hard, and learn from your superiors. Repeat this with a few different fields of sufficient diversity and you'll be in great shape to start a company.

STARTUP IDEAS

Look for an unsexy industry that is behind on the technology adoption curve and then start a company that applies methods from more current industries to the archaic one. For example, you could build many companies based on applying the cutting edge predictive analytics and data mining techniques commonly used at consumer web startups, quantitative hedge funds, etc., to less advanced industries.

The Nine Key Elements of Hands-On Startup Creation.

John R. Frank
Co-Founder, MetaCarta
Co-Founder, Diffeo

#1 LEADING A STARTUP IS LIKE HIKING A SWITCHBACK TRAIL UP A STEEP SLOPE.

After you've hiked in one direction with laser focus, a near 180-degree turn can actually take you higher. Pivoting at the right moments should be part of the plan.

After focusing on MetaCarta's machine learning models for enterprise data, we observed an upswing in consumer-oriented mapping. We pivoted and created OpenLayers, which is now the de facto standard for HTML5 open source mapping. Ultimately, MetaCarta was acquired by Nokia.

#2 LET THE SOCRATES PATTERN BE YOUR GUIDE.

"Surround yourself with brilliant people." - Rick Frank
(Class of '66, and my father)

Few might have ever heard of Socrates if he hadn't surrounded himself with the likes of Plato. Find your Platos. Find them for your team and also in your customers. A startup's first dozen customers leave a long-lasting imprint, so find smart customers who will work with you in making your product useful to them.

#3 OBSERVE EXCELLENCE.

It is difficult to invent or even recognize excellence if you haven't already seen that kind of excellence up close. My appreciation for product design was forever changed by a brief internship at IDEO, one of the world's preeminent design firms.

Let excellence guide your choice of co-founders, advisors, employees, and personal experiences. In selecting team members and investors ask the question: Have they seen excellence in the kinds of activities that matter to your company?

#4 ESTABLISH PRINCIPLES FOR YOUR TEAM

A shared set of principles can help everyone prioritize their actions as they create an enterprise out of an idea. Simple statements such as "Customers come first" and "Style is everything" work best. Challenging situations can bring out the best and worst in people. Cultivate a shared style within your team, so that when under pressure, teammates can reinforce each other with common principles of engagement and shared responsibilities. The best teams exude an aura of humanness and respect for others that does not happen by accident—it starts with the team's leaders.

#5 DIVE INTO EVERY JOB THE COMPANY NEEDS AND DO IT YOURSELF FIRST.

As you grow the team, replace yourself with people who do it better. If you learn the ins and outs of the job from working in that role yourself, you'll know how to hire the right people and how to lead them. This is particularly true for externally-facing roles such as sales—you should close the first dozen deals in any new category or market yourself. Even with the help of excellent coaches and advisors, working with customers yourself will teach you crucial insights that cannot be gained secondhand.

A good rule of thumb: don't hand off sales responsibility to a hired salesperson in your first market or any new market until their entire next twelve months of quota are above ninety percent probability, i.e., approved by the deal lead and going into the customer's procurement process.

#6 PURIFY YOUR PRODUCT.

I prefer this positive statement to the phrase "minimum viable product" because purifying a small set of features is in no way minimalistic. Rather, it means lavishing all your effort on the most high-impact and new-to-the-world elements. Focusing your team's energy on just a few features will clarify their purpose and make them shine.

#7 GIVE AWAY YOUR IDEAS FREELY.

Defending secrets takes effort. Open projects can gain momentum rapidly. Choose wisely what you keep as proprietary. Your first idea will not be your last, and your best idea will probably emerge through discussions with other people.

Cultivate communities around open projects like MetaCarta did with OpenLayers and Diffeo does with TREC. Consider building communities around not-for-profit projects that amplify your mission. Thoughtfully-constructed open projects can shift markets in new directions.

Similarly, cultivating communities of interest with conferences and open contests can crowdsource innovation and advance the state-of-the-art in technologies that your company needs. For example, Diffeo supports NIST's Text Retrieval Conference (TREC) in running an annual contest for inventing algorithms that automatically suggest edits to knowledge bases like Wikipedia.

#8 THERE IS NO NET RISK.

Convince yourself that pursuing your boldest idea has no net risk. Pursuing a bold idea is a worthy end in itself that offsets the risk of failure. By understanding the rewards of the process itself, you will gain the ability to see the forest from deep within the trees. This is particularly true of timing: you can't control the timing of world events that affect your startup, so just jump in with both feet and see what unfolds. Worst-case scenario, you'll learn orders of magnitude more than anyone can learn from the sidelines.

Embracing boldness for its own sake gave us the courage to engage the largest companies in the world as customers, partners, and ultimately acquirers. The bidding war that culminated in MetaCarta's acquisition by Nokia involved two kinds of luck: the reliable kind of luck that comes from hard work and the real luck that occasionally appears when you least expect it.

#9 "80% OF LIFE IS SHOWING UP." ~WOODY ALLEN

Every time I've successfully entered a new market or closed a big deal, it was the direct result of showing up in person at a new place. For example, MetaCarta entered the oil industry after I took my first-ever trip to Texas to attend a randomly-selected conference about data interchange in big oil companies. When I arrived, I was dismayed to discover that it was a twenty-person micro-conference. Then I met our future lead investor, a large customer from Chevron Texaco.

On a more personal note, I met my wife during an impromptu trip to Washington, D.C., for a friend's birthday party. My schedule was packed, so I flew in just for the night. I was on the ground for eleven hours, and that was long enough to start the most important connection of my life.

ADVICE
- for -

SEED
STAGE

TECH
Startups

Advice for Seed Stage Tech Startups.

Michael Seibel
Co-Founder and CEO, Socialcam and Justin.tv

MY FIRST PIECE OF ADVICE CONCERNS YOUR TEAM. An ideal team size for an early-stage tech company is two to four co-founders. These co-founders should have more than six months' previous experience with each other (either as friends or as work colleagues). The team must all be located in the same city (ideally the same apartment), must work on the startup full-time, and must have strong technical ability (50% or more engineers).

The second piece of advice concerns how your company is legally organized. You should either use a tech-focused legal service (like Clerky) or a well-known startup law firm (like WSGR) to incorporate in Delaware. I highly recommend you incorporate as a C corporation and divide equity evenly between the co-founders. Finally, co-founder equity must be vesting (four-year vesting with one year cliff is standard).

My last piece of advice is to launch as soon as possible. You should be looking to build an MVP (minimal viable product). Most MVPs can be built in less than one month. Understand that your first product will not be successful—but it is your responsibility to launch it quickly and to start getting feedback from users. Only then can you start down the road of making something people want.

Have Passion and Be Meticulous.

William (Bill) D. Evers
Chair & General Counsel, Annuvia

AS A LAWYER AND MENTOR ADVISING STARTUPS FOR over fifty years, primarily as to structuring and financing, here are the lessons I learned that I can pass on to Yale entrepreneurs:

GENERAL OBSERVATION

In a startup, you have to have a passion for the correctness, the logic, of what you are undertaking. That is an essential element of any attempt to get others to work for you and/or invest. You also have to be meticulous in preparing your plans, your plea for funding, and finally, in running the business. Those who are sloppy, fail.

LESSON ONE

When selecting what type of entity to use for your business, keep in mind that a Limited Liability Company (frequently pushed by attorneys), does have the short-term advantage of providing the founders and investors with the write-offs of the early losses of the business, BUT, that means that when the business becomes profitable and needs cash for its payables, there is no tax-loss shelter available, so taxes are owed just when cash is needed. Generally, a "C" corporation is the way to go.

Many entrepreneurs choose to incorporate in Delaware. This isn't always wise. It usually means you pay taxes (based on par value in Delaware) and in your home state. Delaware is fine for large companies with management reason, but the best route is to incorporate in your home state and later, if appropriate, reincorporate in Delaware.

Back to the LLC choice, if the business plans to stay small, an LLC does provide great flexibility in ownership rights regarding payout and voting. For instance, the founder can have all the voting power (in most states) and only have a small stake in the profits.

LESSON TWO

Recognize the difference between a business plan that shows your plans for your company and doesn't deal with pie slicing and a Private Placement Memorandum ("PPM") that SHOULD BE designed to cover the following in detail, after a one- or two-page "Elevator Pitch" that summarizes: 1) How much do we want? 2) What will we do with it? 3) What's in it for the investor, and 4) How does the investor get out? These are the really substantive questions on the investor's mind.

The Elevator Pitch should be designed to "hook" the investor psychologically (Wow! I can make some real money on this one!), so he/she will take the time to read the PPM. In the PPM, don't dwell on the detailed technology of your product/service, despite your love and/or pride in it. The investor is only mildly interested in "how" you achieve your product or service, but is very interested in what it does for the customer. If thinking of crowdfunding or Kickstarter, be careful—this is shifting territory as the SEC is still working on the regulations to the Jobs Act.

LESSON THREE

Get a good Board of Directors of at least five members that is not made up of just employees and family. Be sure to MEET AT LEAST ONCE A MONTH for a year or so. This provides a very vital discipline and avoids the problem of the shortcomings of management being ignored and exacerbated. This is the most important lesson.

LESSON FOUR

Keep meticulous records from the get-go. Those with sloppy records invariably fail. In particular, know your cash flow needs every day. And, speaking of cash, keep overhead as low as possible as long as possible. No fancy car rentals, etc.

LESSON FIVE

Try to have as many customers as possible—don't be dependent on one major account.*

---

* Note: This advice is not intended to be legal advice. Entrepreneurs should check whatever they do with their attorneys and accountants.

Fundamental Self-Confidence.

Paul Gu
Co-Founder and Head of Product, Upstart

I LEFT YALE IN THE SPRING OF 2011 TO PURSUE THE Thiel Fellowship. A good friend of mine, a successful Yale entrepreneur himself, told me at the outset that I was making a decision that could ruin my life. I had just spent the summer after my sophomore year working at a highly-selective hedge fund, and, by all indications, was on track for a successful career in finance.

"If you take a couple years to pursue this startup thing, and you *fail*, you'll have a gaping hole on your resume. You're giving up guaranteed wealth and success, and you might find yourself at your five-year class reunion far worse off than your friends expected of you. If that happens, how will you feel then?"

He made the blunt observation that many of the kids from Yale who become entrepreneurs (him included) have family trust funds to fall back on, but I did not.

My friend's words weighed on me often during the next few months. All my life I had been playing a linear game. Get a certain number of A's in "weighted" classes, get a certain SAT score, get into a highly-ranked school, load up on the "right" classes and majors, prepare for every possible job interview brainteaser, land a high-paying job, climb the ladder. Game over.

Starting a company (especially as a first-time entrepreneur) was very different. Not only was there no step-by-step guide to success, but the statistics all said that "most startups fail."

I decided that the risk was worth it. In just the first months of Upstart, I had managed a team, built statistical models, hired employees, and launched a product. I was forced to learn deeper and broader than I ever had before. I was working harder and getting deeper into my work because I loved it at every level of abstraction— the industry, the problem, the product, the people, and the day-to-day. The net result was the fastest pace of personal growth I had ever experienced.

The "hole" that I risked having on my resume was primarily one of signal, not skill. And while perception can trump ability in the short-run, I fundamentally believed that real ability is what matters in the long-run.

Seen in that light, I wasn't taking on more risk. I was taking the surest path (for me) to success.

The Value of Preparation.

Roger McNamee
Co-Founder, Moonalice,
Co-Founder, Elevation Partners, Silver Lake Partners, Integral Capital Partners
Co-Founder, The MoonTunes Project, Reverb

EVERY ENTREPRENEUR'S BODY IS COVERED WITH scar tissue from lessons learned. Even the best startups have setbacks, which means that entrepreneurship is a test of the ability to recover gracefully from mistakes. Entrepreneurs who learn from the experience of others before they start making their own mistakes have a huge advantage.

One major factor in the success of my startups has been preparation. I am a cautious entrepreneur and typically devote at least a year to studying each opportunity before I pursue it. My goal is to be THE domain expert in the field. Almost every startup must find a way to neutralize the advantages of established companies; sometimes the established companies commit suicide, but more often they adapt to new threats.

Preparation doesn't allow entrepreneurs to predict the future, but it does allow them to anticipate the key challenges and be ready for them. This level of preparation has a cost in terms of time, but that is trivial in comparison to the benefits of sidestepping half-baked ideas.

Many entrepreneurs discount the value of preparation in disruptive technology startups on the theory that if you are inventing a new world, you are better off approaching it unfettered by preconceptions. Some investors have stopped backing companies with experienced teams, believing that disruptive change comes most often from first-time entrepreneurs. That was certainly true with Microsoft, Oracle, Google, and Facebook, but the other side of the ledger includes tens of thousands of companies that crashed and burned because of inexperience.

What is the best way to begin an entrepreneurial project? If you are not a domain expert, become one before you start. Domain expertise gives you an edge in identifying product or business model changes that customers will value. It also enables you to "make new mistakes," rather than repeating ones that have been made by others. Once you identify your opportunity, then you have to figure out whether or not you are capable of executing the strategy. This requires self-awareness, which is not as widely distributed in the entrepreneurial population as one would hope. At this early stage, uncertainty has value, as it provides an incentive for greater preparation.

Then comes the moment of truth. You've got your idea; you have a plan for making it happen. Should you do it? My rule of thumb is to sleep on it for a few nights. When you awake, if you can't imagine doing anything else, then you are good to go. If you can imagine anything at all that you would rather do, bail out from the start¬up. It's not the right thing for you. Remember that startups are harder to unwind than a marriage. If you make the wrong choice, you will be stuck with it longer than you would like.

Making an Adventure of Your New Venture.

Peter S. H. Grubstein
Founder and Executive Managing Director, NGEN Partners, LLC

STARTING A COMPANY IS AKIN TO A BUMBLEBEE. Aeronautically, you can't fly, but you do! The most important part of starting a company is not your safety belt, but rather your dream. It is so important that you have fully visualized what you want to do and where you expect to be in 90 days, 180 days, a year, and 5 years from the time you start. To this day, I still do it!

For me, the easiest way to realize my dreams was to actually write down my quarterly goals at the beginning of each quarter, and then to read and reassess at the end of the quarter. As I started my company by myself, this gave me the positive feedback that we all need. I was able at the same time to pat myself on the back and kick myself in the rear. I used a similar annual list. Though lists might sound a bit compulsive, I found I generally exceeded my goals, even if they sometimes took a bit longer to achieve, and it helped perfect my ability to make projections and budgets.

I find that one of the best ways to judge success is how well you are able to project your business. As the entrepreneur, the best way to meet your projections is to really think about your assumptions and be sure that you have included every possible eventuality. As a checklist, I always used the key line items on both sides of the balance sheet. By asking a question on each item, I could thoroughly check the assumptions. For example, when looking at Accounts Receivable I would ask the following questions:

⇨ *Who are the customers?*

⇨ *What is the expected concentration?*

⇨ *Are there sales commissions?*

⇨ *What is the cost of the distribution model?*

⇨ *How quickly do customers pay and how often do the customers reorder?*

This simple set of questions—and there are more for both AR and every line item—directly affects your revenues, cash flow, and sales expenses. They also provide great insight into the accuracy of your projections.

The last simple piece of advice is to build systems infrastructure immediately. Make sure you have all the database type aids possible, so you can automate the interaction between sales, marketing, and production (even if for awhile that is all the same person). Simple CRM (customer relation management) software, so long as it is relational, is all you need at first. You can customize it easily, but this allows you to be much more productive without adding people.

Therefore, the inverse is equally important. Don't add too many people before they can be productive, even if you can afford them. Once you are sure they will be productive, add the people.

Outlook.

Miles Lasater
Founder, Higher One
Founder, SeeClickFix
Founder, Yale Entrepreneurial Society

OUTLOOK

Within a startup
Team has future optimism
Pessimism re: now

FOR WANT OF A CUSTOMER

Grow users! More cash flow! 's my creed.
And to get it, a product I need.

Employees want salary, to build.
To pay, I must woo VC guild.
But investors seek traction indeed!

THE BENEFIT OF CO-FOUNDERS

With a co-founder,
highs and lows in startup land
hit each off-cycle.

BEGIN NOW

A startup, like a
sailboat, can only rightly
steer when moving. Start!

BECOMING AN ENTREPRENEUR.

Advice from a Professor to Young Entrepreneurs.

Barry Nalebuff

Milton Steinbach Professor, Yale School of Management

Co-Founder, Honest Tea

WE WERE THIRSTY. WE COULDN'T FIND ANYTHING we wanted to drink, so we started a company to make bottled iced tea that actually tasted like tea. My former student Seth Goldman and I started out with five thermoses, and from there we grew Honest Tea to annual sales of $70 million in 2011, the year Coca-Cola purchased the company.

As a result, quite a few young entrepreneurs find their way to my door, asking for advice. Here's my advice: Don't do it. Or, at least wait.

If you're concerned I'm sounding negative, it's just that I don't think young entrepreneurs need any additional encouragement. If anything, they tend to be overconfident and unable to imagine all the things that can go wrong or appreciate all the things that have to go right. If I can talk someone out of proceeding, then he or she likely didn't have the conviction and passion required to get them through.

There's no rush to pull the trigger. For most entrepreneurs, their first idea is unlikely to be the best idea of their life. Of course, there are exceptions; undergraduates are often uniquely qualified to see the potential for web-based businesses, especially ones designed for their friends. That said, I've seen students give up a good portion of their bright college years trying to build a catering business, a t-shirt printing company, and even a vending machine for umbrellas. This is a fine alternative to a campus job in the library. But don't lose perspective: think of it as a job, not something worth dropping out for, or even missing classes for.

What then is a young would-be entrepreneur to do? One option is to learn on someone else's dime. Join another startup to see first-hand what they do right and wrong. Be forewarned: Having worked for a startup, you may find it hard to ever go back to corporate America. It's not that employers don't value entrepreneurial experience— they usually see it as an asset—but after making things happen in a fast-paced startup environment, you may not have the patience for the bureaucracy of a corporate setting.

In a world where Peter Thiel is bribing students to drop out of college to pursue their startup dreams, allow me to make a shameless plug for my day job teaching MBAs. The normal course of education is to become increasingly specialized. An English major starts out reading fiction, non-fiction, poetry, and plays. Over time, he or she focuses on 20th Century literature, then Virginia Woolf, and finally on Mrs. Dalloway and her flowers. Most graduate schools train you to be a specialist. Business school is just the opposite. We require our students to take classes in accounting, economics, finance, marketing, negotiation, operations, organization behavior, and strategy. We force students to take courses outside their comfort zone.

The challenge in leading a startup is you have to be a jack of all trades, and master of many. If you don't know enough about an area, you are bound to make mistakes, and the business world is unforgiving. Even small mistakes can be fatal. Sure you can hire experts, but if you don't really understand the field, you'll have trouble hiring and managing the right talent.

While it's easy to idealize the fun and rewarding aspects of building a company, the dangers are harder to imagine. Yes, I want you to live out your passion—and make the world a better place. But I also want you to succeed.*

---

* This essay is adapted from *Mission in a Bottle*, Barry Nalebuff's book co-written with Seth Goldman on the history of Honest Tea.

Is Entrepreneurship for You?

Fritz Lanman
Founder, Livestar
Angel Investor, Square, Pinterest, etc.

ENTREPRENEURSHIP IS THE HEART OF CAPITALISM and the lifeblood of the American economy; there is no nobler profession or more honorable pursuit. That said, it's really hard to build a successful business, and it's a terrible profession to choose unless you cannot live to do anything else.

There are no rules or frameworks to guide you, and doing is the only way to learn. The best thing you can do is put yourself in environments where you maximize your chances of success; develop the skills that are necessary (programming, basic finance, product expertise, market analysis, structured/effective communication, etc.), find a way to meet people who have useful perspective/contacts. You've got to write your own story.

If you want to experience heightened survival senses—and have the chance to achieve greatness—then become an entrepreneur. But for god's sake, don't do it for the money (as the odds are stacked against you) or because you want to "experience" it; only do it if there is something that you cannot stand to see the world live without.

The Basics.

Kathy Moskal
Co-Founder, HUE
Founder, VERE
Founder, OKOKO

THERE ARE DIFFERENT TYPES OF ENTREPRENEURS (see Wikipedia). This may seem obvious, but know which type you are. It will help you focus and make better decisions regarding what you wish to accomplish.

Keep your suppliers informed regarding payments if they will be late. This builds real trust and a feeling of fellowship that can often be more valuable than a financial statement, especially when you're starting out.

STEAL
SHAMELESSLY

A To-Do List for the Aspiring Entrepreneur.

Casey Gerald
Co-Founder and CEO, MBAs Across America

FROM MY PERCH AT HARVARD BUSINESS SCHOOL, I can tell you one thing about the future of American business: it will be built by entrepreneurs with great visions and real grit, not just a fancy MBA. Before you change the world, though, there are a few things that you should do, which I have learned from my early career and the experiences of other dreamers and doers across America.

#1 ASK YOURSELF: ARE YOU AN ENTREPRENEUR?

A wise man (Jay Z) once said, "It ain't for everybody." He was right, and it doesn't have to be. Being an entrepreneur is *en vogue*, but doing it for the wrong reasons can be just as bad as, or worse than, not doing it at all. My two-part test:

⇨ Do you have a great idea?
⇨ Are you working with someone you are convinced is extraordinary AND sane?

If neither of these conditions is met, go get a great job. If you have one of the two, consider taking a chance. If you have both, you can really make magic happen.

#2 JUMP...AND DON'T HAVE ANYTHING TO FALL BACK ON.

So often we stand at the threshold of doing something truly great, something we were put on this earth to do, and we let fear—both of failure and of success—stop us dead in our tracks. The great difficulty, someone wrote, is to say "yes" to life. But at some point we all will die and there will be nothing left to say yes to. Do it now.

When Wynton Marsalis decided to jump and become a jazz musician, his father told him, "Don't ever have something to fall back on, because you'll fall back." I've found the same to be true when it comes to starting a project, movement, or company. If you're not 100% in, you might as well not be in at all. So put your McKinsey cover letter away—consulting will always be around; your unique opportunity to change the world may not.

#3 STOP READING MANAGEMENT BOOKS.

The first thing I did when I was hired to help run a startup was go out and buy three or four books on business and management—from *The First 90 Days*, to *Reality Check*—devouring them and taking copious notes that I planned to use on day one. Day one came and I never saw the notes again, not because the books weren't great, but because they had very little to do with the daily grind of getting things done. Books help us do a lot of things, but they don't hire people or get new clients, so focus on that and then give Jim Collins a call.

#4 FORGET THAT YOU WENT TO YALE.

I know, this defeats the whole purpose of going to Yale in the first place. But if you're going to change the world and be a non-obnoxious person while you're doing it, you're going to have to eat a few slices of humble pie and acknowledge the fact that nobody cares where you went to school if you have a great idea and a kickass team. This is a good thing. Listen more. Brag less. Retire your blue blazer and khaki pants—there's always your twenty-year reunion for you to pull them out again.

#5 STAY OUT OF DEBT.

For 5,000 years, debt has been ruining empires and individuals alike. Don't let it ruin your freedom and flexibility. Pay back the loans you already have as quickly as possible. Be frugal. Shop sales. Learn how to cook, or at least how to make a good sandwich. Throw away all the credit card offers you get in the mail. Don't spend a quarter of a million dollars on business school. Read Napoleon Hill's chapter in *The Law of Success* on personal debt, and thank me later.

#6 STEAL SHAMELESSLY.

The first Christians stole half of a book from Judaism. The founding fathers stole ideas from the British, the Romans, and Enlightenment philosophers. Even The Beatles stole! If it was good enough for Jesus, George Washington, and Paul McCartney, it's good enough for you. As you try to make something out of your great idea and kickass team, don't waste time trying to reinvent the wheel. Use the wheels that already exist and invent something else. Austin Kleon's book, *Steal Like an Artist*, is a great guide to stealing in the most productive, ethical way possible.

#7 WRITE A STORY, NOT A BUSINESS PLAN.

You know how to write a business plan—tell them the problem;

tell them how you solve it; tell them how you'll make money; etc.—and you've done tons of research to figure out how to pack as much data into a presentation that will hopefully impress investors before it bores them to death. Great.

But every other entrepreneur worth her salt will have this too. What will set you apart is a story—the "why" to all the "whats" of your business plan. Not because people don't care about facts. Not because the data doesn't matter. Tell me a story because I want to envision a future that is drastically better than the past and the present. Tell me a story because the facts and the data can change. Tell me a story because your brand has to be more than just a set of products or services that people pay you for—it has to enable those you serve to be better, to be whole, to be great. Otherwise, it's just a twenty-page presentation with no life and no chance of changing the world.

One idea: write your deck with a Sharpie on twenty pieces of blank paper. Write in large letters so you can only fit the most compelling and important line or two on the page. We're most creative when we're active, so keep drafting until you're exhausted and your story makes somebody cry.

#8 FIND CHAMPIONS, NOT MENTORS.

A politician friend of mine who is trying to build a private law practice told me not long ago, "I'm advice-d out." I totally understood what he was saying. You're a bright, interesting person, who may or may not do something cool in the world. Lots of folks will set aside thirty minutes on their calendar to talk to you—they might even buy you a meal and introduce you to one of their friends. These people often become mentors, and you should cherish them.

But what you need right now is a champion, someone who is out there advocating on your behalf—getting their friends to give you free legal advice, having a serious conversation about seed funding, telling you when you screw up and helping you fix it. Learn how to tell the difference between the two, and save yourself a lot of time that you could spend getting things done.

One note here: never be a user and don't burn bridges. Look for win-wins and be genuine in your interactions. Your most valuable asset is your reputation and no startup is worth ruining that.

#9 WIN THE WAR.

Entrepreneurship, like life, isn't easy or fair. You will make mistakes. You will be disappointed. You may even fail. But if you look at any great figure or effort in the history of mankind, you will see that these mistakes, failures, and heartaches were central to a final triumph. Your failures are commas, not periods, so don't give up every time you lose a battle—just win the bloody war.

Bonus: Post this quote on your desk or wall and read it every time somebody thinks (or you think yourself) that you're finished:

"It is not the critic who counts; not the man who points out how the strong man stumbles, or where the doer of deeds could have done them better. The credit belongs to the man who is actually in the arena, whose face is marred by dust and sweat and blood; who strives valiantly; who errs, who comes short again and again, because there is no effort without error and shortcoming; but who does actually strive to do the deeds; who knows great enthusiasms, the great devotions; who spends himself in a worthy cause; who at the best knows in the end the triumph of high achievement, and who at the worst, if he fails, at least fails while daring greatly, so that his place shall never be with those cold and timid souls who neither know victory nor defeat." ~Teddy Roosevelt

Good luck and Godspeed!

An Entrepreneur's Luck.

Donna Dubinsky
Co-Founder, Palm
Co-Founder, Handspring
Co-Founder, Numenta

WHEN I WAS A STUDENT AT YALE, THERE WAS NO WAY I could have imagined where I would end up: as CEO of a public, high-technology company and as a participant in four major computing revolutions: personal computing, handheld computing, smartphones, and intelligent computing. Heck, I was a history major!

How did this happen? Some days I think to myself that I was awfully lucky. I had the right mentors and met the right people and managed to hang on. Was I just in the "right place at the right time"?

Well, to be sure, there was some luck involved. It happened that the Philadelphia National Bank was recruiting at Yale, and they gave me my first job as a financial analyst, where I fell in love with the business world. It happened that the creators of Visicalc gave a presentation at my business school, a moment that changed my life and introduced me to the idea of personal computers. It happened that when I went to work at Apple, I ended up working for great bosses, who taught me a lot about management. It happened that one of my mentors left to create a new company and called me to come along.

After another few years, it happened that I met Jeff Hawkins, who had just created Palm, when I was anxious to step into the CEO role, and he happened to pick me. It happened that the technology had advanced sufficiently such that we were able to create the first generation of handheld computers and, subsequently, smartphones.

Did these things just "happen"? Or was there more than luck involved?

If I had to give one piece of advice, I'd say this: put yourself in situations that allow luck to happen, recognize it when it does, and take best advantage. Pay attention and lay the groundwork. Be ready.

Going back to that "aha" moment when I understood that we all would be using a personal computer (this may seem obvious now, but it was not the least bit obvious in 1981), I made a vow to go to work for Apple Computer. I had seen the future, and I wanted to be a part of it. Since I did not have a technical degree, I was not accepted for an interview on campus, so I sat outside the interviewer's office all day, politely letting her know that I was available to chat whenever she had a minute. Finally, she relented, and I explained that Apple also needed non-technical people who could work with customers, and, eventually, I ended up with a job in customer support, launching my high-tech career. Luck? Well, learning about Apple at that moment was lucky for me, but persistence is what got me the job.

In another example, I met Jeff Hawkins through Silicon Valley networking. I was seeking a CEO position, and he was looking for a CEO. When I met him, I immediately was inspired by his vision of the next generation of computing, handheld computing. But, would he pick me? I gave him a page full of references: people I'd worked for, people I'd worked with, people who had reported to me. I always had been careful to build great relationships. I had a personal goal that everybody who worked with me would be willing to work with me again. Even if things didn't go well in some aspect of the business, I tried to be respectful and professional.

Well, those many years of relationship building paid off. Jeff called my extensive list, dug around for a few of his own, and consistently heard positive feedback. He hired me, and I've been privileged to work in partnership with him for over twenty years and three companies.

Yes, I've been very lucky. And I recommend that you try to be lucky, too! But, I also know this—luck doesn't just happen, it happens to those who are looking for it. As it is often said, luck is the marriage of preparation and opportunity.

Can Entrepreneurs Actually Be Advised?

Jeffrey Brenzel
Master of Timothy Dwight College, Yale University
Lecturer, Philosophy Department, Yale University

THE TROUBLE WITH ADVICE WHEN STARTING OUT AS an entrepreneur is that entrepreneurs self-select for an unusual degree of inner direction and stubborn persistence in their own ideas. That is, they see most clearly the thing they wish to pursue or accomplish or bring into being, and have a hard time taking into account anything else.

A good venture capitalist friend told me that in his forty years of financing entrepreneurs, he has never met a single one whose business plan projections were anything but utopian. This is not to say that entrepreneurs are either dumb or manipulative. It is only to say that unless they were wild-eyed optimists with blinders on, the daunting realities of starting a business would probably keep them from being entrepreneurs to begin with.

An entrepreneur is also inevitably subjected to much advice of every kind, both good and bad. Even if a particular entrepreneur were more receptive to advice in general, he or she would face the distinct challenge of discerning what advice was both wise and timely.

So as I think back to the venture I launched myself, and to the other startups in which I participated as an employee or principal, I do not find it hard to imagine the good advice that would have benefited me. I only have a hard time imagining that I would have paid proper attention to it.

If the question, rather, is what I *learned* from starting, financing, and building a business, then I think there is absolutely no substitute in the making of an entrepreneur for experience of both failure and success. I therefore believe that the best path to entrepreneurship is working for other peoples' startups and early-stage companies before trying to launch one of your own.

The Entrepreneurial Life.

Mark Gerson
Co-Founder and Chairman, Gerson Lehrman Group
Co-Founder and Chairman, Thuzio
Chairman, United Hatzalah
Chairman, African Mission Healthcare Foundation

PERHAPS ONE OF THE MOST FUNDAMENTAL MIS-takes new entrepreneurs make is when they don't share their ideas out of concern that those ideas will be stolen. The risk of larceny certainly exists, but it is unquestionably outweighed—on a risk-adjusted basis—by the benefits that accrue through sharing. Sharing an idea will often result in its refinement. Fundamental and very helpful questions about its viability are often brought forth as well as relationships that can help to bring the idea to fruition. In general, there can be lots of positive outcomes.

Stealing an idea, however, requires the thief to drop what he is doing, recruit a team to join him, and beat the person with the idea to market. Starting a business has risk all around it. The entrepreneur must embrace risk as a job requirement, and this is just one of many (and perhaps the one whose uncertainty is most likely to lead to positive rather than negative outcomes).

Another common mistake results from misunderstanding risk altogether. Of course, starting a business involves risk—seen and unseen, predictable and completely surprising—but so do most activities. Working at a larger institution may seem less "risky," but a significant downsizing might be in the near offing and economic or political forces (both internal and external to the organization) beyond the control of an individual can determine his fate. So whether or not one pursues an entrepreneurial opportunity should be taken with full awareness that while its risks may be well-known, the risks in any alternative can be just as real, if not just as obvious.

Once the decision to pursue the entrepreneurial life is made, a third category of mistake often results—that derived from the commercial goal of the business. There is only one commercial goal, and that is long-term sustainability. Entrepreneurship is a race of time against money, and therefore a clear plan towards profitability must be articulated. It is fine if the plan changes, so long as the new plan is always clear as to how the business will become profitable. To think that it doesn't matter because the business will be of "strategic" value to an acquirer—or a similar (in some sense) business sold without being profitable—introduces an element of risk that is simply unacceptable; it transforms what should be business building into a form of the lottery (with a negative expected return).

When an idea is conceived, and its path to profitability can be articulated, it is crucial that another grand mistake be avoided—the lack of radical honesty. For instance, many entrepreneurs say that their business "has no competitors." Usually, they are just defining competitor too narrowly—often, as another company that does exactly what they are proposing to do (rather than another company with a claim on their would-be customer's dollar).

A related problem is when entrepreneurs ask their friends for their input and report a universally positive response. This might be masking that their friends are just being "polite," or at least avoiding conflict, or even just disappointing a friend. Praise is cheap and easy. Spending real money is neither. And that (or as close as one can come to that, given the state of the business's development) is a far better test of an idea's validity.

The entrepreneurial life can be a wonderful thing, and the chances of it being fulfilling in every sense can be enhanced through radical honesty (and the direct seeking of it), a sober assessment of risk (and a willingness to embrace it), and a willingness to share and to learn (and to incorporate the benefits of so doing into one's plans and actions).

GROWING OUTSIDE

YOUR COMFORT ZONE

Growing Out of Your Comfort Zone.

Victor Cheng
Co-Founder and CTO, PaperG

PEOPLE OFTEN ROMANTICIZE THE IDEA OF START-ups—they think you get to work on your own ideas on your own time with your own methods, and eventually make it big. Unfortunately the reality is that, as with many romanticizations, the dreams of grandeur gloss over the hard work required. Entrepreneurship will involve doing some of what you want to do, but it also involves doing a lot of what you don't want to do. However, it's a great learning experience that can prepare you for many different roles in the future by forcing you to constantly get out of your comfort zone.

Beginning as an introverted green engineer, I learned about many things along the way—new technology was the only expected area. I unexpectedly also learned about interviewing people, managing older people with more experience, building a team, selling/ pitching, explaining technology to laymen—the list of knowledge and skills I had unintentionally picked up is huge and extends beyond this.

For example, in the first summer of PaperG, my main focus was to build our first product, Flyerboard. I was excited because I thought I would be able to dig straight in and start programming, which was all I really wanted to do. I thought I would just have to master PHP and Flash, but soon learned I would have to pick up MySQL, ActionScript, JavaScript, and a slew of other software involving system administration and setting up servers.

Luckily, I had a great group of co-founders who could take care of most of the business side. However, I still needed to learn a decent amount about it as well, because it's important to take the business concerns into account as you build a product. At the same time, I had to learn to describe my technical decisions in non-technical terms so that partners could understand a bit more of what was happening and to give them assurance that we knew what we were doing. As the company grew, I spent less time programming and more time managing, figuring out hiring (both always more troublesome for the introvert in me), and doing research about possible directions for the company and our technology.

Most of this time was spent out of my comfort zone, acquiring knowledge I would have rarely encountered in a corporation like Microsoft or Google, but it's made me well-rounded in my understanding of a business as a whole and helped me figure out what aspects of the tech world I enjoy the most.

Large companies don't need you—small companies do. This forces you to learn skills you might not have dealt with simply because your company won't survive otherwise. It's often helpful in life to be exposed to experiences we might not otherwise desire, because it's usually in those situations that we learn the most. You'll also gain a greater appreciation for the things that you do enjoy doing, rather than take them for granted.

Trust—The Way To Overcome Uncertainty.

Patricia Brett
Founder and Designer, Veronica Brett

FOR ME, THE LIFE OF AN ENTREPRENEUR CAN BE summed up in one word: uncertainty. *Will my idea work? Will people buy it? Can I do it? Where will I get the money? Should I quit my day job? Etc., etc., etc.*

If we stop to *really* consider all those issues, we entrepreneurs could hold ourselves back forever. Yes, there must be a market analysis, an understanding of the ideal price point, an assessment of our skills (or lack thereof), and potential investors to consider. However, at some point we just have to take the leap.

There will always be unknowns, things we didn't take into consideration and roadblocks (or land mines!) that obstruct our way forward. If we wait until the stars are in perfect alignment and we know all the answers, chances are someone else will have beaten us to it, our idea will have become outdated, or we will have simply lost steam.

At some point, you just have to jump into your endeavor and trust that it will all work.

I truly believe that we succeed when we act based on our own positive and limitless thoughts. The challenge is the necessary continual focus on the positive.

To keep myself moving forward while establishing Veronica Brett, I kept a small journal in which I recorded my thoughts and successes as well as the stumbling blocks. The act of putting everything on paper allowed me to celebrate (and remember!) my achievements; while relegating the not-so-great events to paper allowed me to put them behind me, to put them to rest.

I keep my "clarity journal" in a small weekly Moleskin planner, with my (+) list on the left-hand side and my (–) list on the right-hand side of each page. In addition to my notes, I collect bits of inspiration and write them in the empty back pages of the journal. When the going gets rough, I flip back and read a few bits of inspiration to remind me to trust: trust in myself, my idea, and the knowledge that somehow it will all work out.

Some of the quotes are religious, and others I'm certain I simplified/adopted as I jotted them down. The following are a few favorites that keep me going. (I have credited them where I can.)

"I am not afraid ... I was born to do this!" ~Jean de Arc

"The secret ingredient (in secret ingredient soup) is you!" ~From (loosely) the movie Kung Fu Panda (What can I say, I'm the mom of a young boy! This movie is one of my all-time favorites and a great reminder to believe in ourselves.)

"Life is this simple: we are living in a world that is absolutely transparent and the divine is shining through it all the time." ~Thomas Merton

"Today is the day and you are the team." ~Motto of the Notre Dame fighting Irish football team (as seen on the back of a t-shirt).

"Ask to have peace of mind and heart no matter what life brings

you." ~Fr. William J. Bergen, S.J. (in a sermon delivered at the Church of St. Ignatius Loyola, NYC).

And finally from one of my favorite authors, Vietnamese monk, Thich Nhat Hanh, in his book, *You Are Here*:

> "Has the most wonderful moment of your life already happened? ... The teaching of the Buddha tells you clearly and plainly to make this the most magnificent and wonderful moment of your life. The present moment must become the most wonderful moment in your life. All you need to transform this present moment into a wonderful one is freedom. All you need to do is free yourself from your worries and preoccupations about the past, the future, and so on."

So, my advice to the young entrepreneur is to figure out what you need to do to provide yourself with the ongoing trust you need to overcome uncertainly. Or, as Nike simply declares, "Just do it!"

The Case for Humility.

Justin Borgman
Founder and CEO, Hadapt, Inc.

EVERY SUCCESSFUL ENTREPRENEUR I KNOW SHARES a few essential characteristics—intelligence, creativity, a tireless work ethic, and perhaps most importantly, a relentless determination to succeed against all odds. These attributes are table stakes for any entrepreneur. You simply cannot survive without them.

But I want to talk about another attribute, a quality that never seems to get the attention it deserves: humility.

In this age of chest-thumping athletes, reality TV divas, blogging, tweeting, Facebooking, and other examples of self-aggrandizement, this simple virtue is often forgotten. And, while it may not be required for success, you will certainly do well to incorporate some humble pie in your diet.

As a first-time entrepreneur, you have to realize from the start that you do not have all the answers. In fact, you do not even know the right questions to ask most of the time. But that is all okay because this is going to be an incredible learning experience. If you approach the company-building process with this attitude, you are going to be more willing to acknowledge your mistakes as they occur and treat them as valuable lessons rather than failures. Believe me, there will be many of these "lessons" along the way.

A commitment to learning and continuous self-improvement yields other benefits as well. It makes you more coach-able, and therefore, more likely to attract great mentors to help you climb that steep learning curve even faster. You will definitely need the help. Sometimes people ask me how I have been able to make it as a young first-time CEO of a fast-growing database company—a feat that is normal in consumer web startups but utterly unheard of in enterprise software. The answer is pretty simple: I surrounded myself with the best of the best and learned everything I could from them. I simply would not be where I am today without their support.

Humility is also contagious, particularly when exhibited by someone in a leadership position. Your company will naturally form a culture that reflects you as the founder and your personal values. So lead by example. Celebrate team accomplishments more than individual achievements. Admit your own mistakes when you make them and hold yourself accountable in the same way that you would everyone else. As a result, you will teach your employees that it is okay to make mistakes as long as you learn from them, and nobody is bigger than the team, not even you.

Ultimately, there are many different paths to success, and it is up to you to decide how you will reach your destination. But before you begin that journey, ask yourself the following question: What kind of entrepreneur do I want to be?

An Entrepreneurial Checklist.

Tobin Fisher
Co-Founder, Sutro Media
Co-Founder, Ardica Technologies

⇨ MAKE SURE THAT YOU ARE DEEPLY PASSIONATE about whatever area you decide to pursue. Consider that it can often take ten years to go from idea to successful exit and that there will very likely be some dark, hard times in that decade. Desire for riches alone will rarely be enough to get you through.

⇨ If you want to be an entrepreneur and you have a general area that you are passionate about, start working on something as if it's "the idea." It probably won't be "the idea," but you generally have to get your hands dirty and your mind deeply into your area (think one year of work) in order to get to a truly good idea. There's no better way to do this than to start working and building something. With this in mind, be prepared to drop your first idea and move on to something better.

⇨ Use your initial work to draw on your networks and build the foundations for new ideas, first employees, and potential investors. These sorts of meetings go much better if you've already done work and built something to show (a business plan doesn't count). This network of people that knows what you're doing and the next steps that you've committed to can often be helpful in motivating you and/ or your team to reach near-term next steps.

⇨ Be humble. Assume that everything you believe to be true may be wrong. The faster you get product in the hands of paying customers the faster you can learn from your inevitable mistakes and correct them.

⇨ Don't do equal partnerships. Even with a board to act as a tie breaker, power struggles between partners seem to arise from the best of relationships and can do irreparable damage to companies.

⇨ Hire slowly and fire quickly. The team you build will make or break your company. Do it very carefully. Bad employees can destroy a company's culture in a blink of an eye—know what's over the line and end bad situations immediately.

⇨ Take care of your team above all else. Per point 3, there's nothing more important than the team. If you are leading the team, think of your role as an enabler of greatness for each of your teammates—never put your accomplishments ahead of theirs. Problems will come and go, but once a team losses faith, morale, or good cultural values, it can be very hard to recover.

⇨ Build a culture of greatness. It's easy to make excuses for being less than great when you're getting going and the chips are stacked against you. Don't do this. It's much easier to always do great work if you never, ever, accept mediocrity. This is in tension with point 2—there's no easy path to striking a balance of greatness and speed, although working really, really hard definitely helps.

JUMP AT

OPPORTUNITY

Jump at Opportunity.

Sander Daniels
Co-Founder, Thumbtack, Inc.

WHEN I WAS AT YALE I NEVER IMAGINED BECOMING an entrepreneur. I had no idea how to start a company, and I never would have done so had I not been good friends with two extremely entrepreneurial people. These two friends dreamt of creating something tangible from nothing but an idea. So they decided to start a company together. They brought me into the loop because I'm a hard worker and a clear thinker. I brainstormed ideas with them, and then they started the company. The door was open for me to join at any time.

At the time I was in law school at Yale. I took only one year off between undergrad and law school, and I had not spent much time in the working world. After law school, I practiced at a law firm for fourteen months. I made a great salary and was happy with my job. However, this new company was becoming more and more promising. To take advantage of the opportunity, I would need to move with my wife and baby to San Francisco and abandon a great, steady salary.

Whether to jump at the opportunity was an extremely difficult decision. My parents questioned my decision, my friends questioned my decision, and, most importantly, I questioned my decision. I had a law degree and a family—could I afford financially to forego a law firm salary and chase after a dream? Would uprooting a comfortable and happy life be worth it to pursue a venture that had a 98% chance of failing?

I finally took the leap and decided to leave my steady job. It turned out to be one of the best decisions I've ever made. I didn't realize this before, but I now know that, other than getting married, having kids, and staying healthy, there is nothing that can make you happier than starting your own company.

Since starting in 2009, we at Thumbtack have grown our company to 900 people worldwide, raised $150 million in funding, and grown our user base to many millions of people. I can't imagine anything more rewarding than creating something new in the world and having people pay you because they like it. Every single dollar that someone spends on our site is money they could have saved or spent elsewhere, and they pay us money only because we have built something new that is better than anything similar. I have learned so much: how to work productively and closely with a team of people for a long time, how thankful people are for creating a job for them that supports their family and their dreams, and that it is possible to create something amazing if you are willing and able to put yourself in a position to determine your own destiny.

As an added but not uncommon bonus, I now work with some of my best friends—two of my best friends from high school and college sit on either side of me at work every day. We determine our own working hours. We determine the company's culture and hiring standards. We are a team creating something great that millions of people use and which wouldn't exist had we not dreamt it.

I was very close to missing out on this opportunity. However, the last-second decision to jump at it opened a whole world of professional fulfillment that I didn't realize existed. I wish I hadn't been so conservative in my early career decisions and had jumped at this opportunity sooner. I didn't realize the intangible benefits of taking risks, and finally doing so has transformed my entire life—personally and professionally—for the better. Seizing the opportunity to help start a company is one of the best decisions I have ever made.

Entrepreneur Your Life.

Gregg Vanourek
Course Director, Stockholm School of Entrepreneurship
Co-Author, *Life Entrepreneurs: Ordinary People Creating Extraordinary Lives*

AS YOU BUILD YOUR STARTUP VENTURE, DON'T FORGET to be the visionary entrepreneur of the other important venture that is unfolding—your life. Startups are white hot with intensity and disconcerting ups and downs. Don't let them consume you.

Ambitious entrepreneurs have a fierce will to succeed. It helps to maintain an overarching vision not only of the venture but also of your life and how the venture fits into it. Be the entrepreneur of your life, not just your venture.

Figure out not only what you want, but *why*. Figure out not only who to hire or partner with, but also who to spend your life with. Figure out not just how to succeed, but how to serve. Iterate your way not only to a business model that works, but also to a life that matters.

Live and lead with a deep and abiding integrity. Entrepreneur your life.

MOTIVES AND MOTIVATION.

Are Entrepreneurs Really the Happiest People on Earth?

Jane Park
CEO and Founder, Julep Beauty

ONE OF THE QUESTIONS I'M ASKED MOST OFTEN IS, "Are you happy all the time because you're an entrepreneur?" The mythology of entrepreneurialism is powerful. You "answer only to yourself," "set the rules," and "make your own decisions." Or so the myth goes, anyway. The leap out of safe, corporate life seems daunting; the assumption is that those who manage to make it over the line must live out their days in self-actualized bliss. More times than I can count, men and women, young and old, have cornered me to ask, "It must be great to be your own boss! Is it everything you ever dreamed it would be?" Thus far, I have had the decency and self-awareness to stop myself short of bursting out laughing. Because, as anyone who has founded a company understands, entrepreneurialism is more like a mental illness than a state of nirvana.

Based on my own experience, and the truthful responses of others I know, here is what it really feels like to be an entrepreneur:

#1 AS TRITE AS IT SOUNDS, YOU FEEL COMPELLED.

You can't stop thinking about your idea and how to make it better 24/7. When you're showering. When you're driving. When you're supposed to be clearing your mind in yoga.

The follow-up question to, "Are you happy all the time?" is often, "When did you know you wanted to leave the safe corporate life and take this huge risk?" I try to explain that none of it happened that way, at least for me. As unromantic as it is, there was no joyful leap like the kind photographed in sports pages or motivational posters. It felt less like a jump and more like a gradual melting away of other plausible alternatives. I just put one foot in front of the other on the only path left. Wiser entrepreneurs have described their founding process as a weary realization that it's what they had to do—in spite of what they knew would be impending pain and heartache.

#2 ENTREPRENEURIALISM IS A NEVER-ENDING LESSON IN HUMILITY.

If you are an effective entrepreneur, you end up hiring people smarter than you are in every function. After all, as a founder, you are always just a "minimally viable product," holding a position only until an expert in the function comes along to relieve you. You also end up reporting to a board smarter than you are, filled with people who have been there before, scaling organizations and keeping track of the signs of peril. Finally, you end up serving consumers who are way smarter than you in knowing exactly what they want. All you can do is commit to collaborating with all these amazing resources to get to the best solutions.

#3 MOST IMPORTANTLY, ENTREPRENEURIALISM FEELS LIKE OPTIMISM.

For me, the most powerful thing about being an entrepreneur is my effort to believe that tomorrow can be better than today. I started Julep because I wanted to create a space for beauty without judgment—where women could be free to explore and share without the crushing pressure to be perfect. Being a woman today is fraught with expectation and anxiety—no woman needs more judgment from her makeup bag. I wanted to build a better way for women to connect and cheer each other on, to have more fun, and to take more risks outside their comfort zones. I also wanted to build a better company, where we treat each other better and come up with better ideas. Entrepreneurialism is about a belief that better is achievable—one step at a time.

I didn't start a company because I wanted freedom, or with the belief I would be jumping out of bed every day bursting in song. Asking the question, "Are you happy because you're an entrepreneur" is the wrong question altogether. I think a more appropriate question is, "Are you making a difference?" And to that I can whole-heartedly answer, "I am trying!" I know for sure that I'm more engaged and connected. And that's what makes it exciting to wake up every day.

Nothing Else.

Patrick Foley, Ph.D.
Chief Science Officer, P2 Science

*A piece of advice—make sure there is
nothing else you would rather be doing.*

ALL ALONG I HAD INTENDED TO GO INTO MEDICINE. For several years after I graduated college I worked in drug discovery as a chemist, weighing my options, and trying to figure out how best to proceed—considering where I should apply, how I should finance it, whether I should do an MD or a PhD or an MD/PhD and, if so, in what field. I spoke with a lot of med students and doctors in an effort to inform my decision—including my cousin Ted, who was doing a plastic surgery residency at the time. Ted and I spoke at length and shared many correspondences, one of which stuck with me. And I'm paraphrasing ...

Ted said, "I work seventy to eighty hours a week, which works out to about $6.75 per hour. I am several hundred thousand dollars in debt, I have been at this for seven years, and I still have years to go before I can practice. I am constantly sleep deprived, and I rarely get

115

to spend time with my family."

"That sounds like plain hell," I said.

"Yeah, in the darkest moments, in the middle of a marathon shift, overtired, sick in a bunch of different ways with another nine hours still to go, you think about your kids, your wife, *and you spend a lot of time thinking about what you would rather be doing with your life*. I think about business, other types of medicine, research, farming … everything. Luckily, for me, I can't think of anything I would rather be doing. Whatever you do, you have to have that."

Ultimately, I did not go into medicine. Although I realize the importance of the discipline, and I completely admire its practitioners, the thoughts Ted left me with made me uncomfortable. Not long after I spoke with Ted, I took a thorough inventory of what I wanted out of life and I began to realize that what I wanted was different. I ended up pursuing my PhD at Yale, not in medicine, but in environmental engineering. I pursued ideas that I felt passionate about, and surrounded myself with people whom I admired and could learn from—people who were looking at some of the world's greatest challenges in creative and daring new ways. It was a challenging transition, but it was completely rewarding.

I have only recently become an entrepreneur, not out of a long-standing desire to start a company, but rather out of a desire to have the right answer to the inherent question Ted posed. From my limited experience, being an entrepreneur is all-consuming. There are certainly fun days and rewarding days, but they are not every day. The hours are long and the work is hard. Setbacks can feel soul crushing. Resources are always strained to the limit. But even in the darkest moments, I am not conflicted. I can feel good, because I know there is nothing else I would rather be doing.

Whatever you do, you have to have that.

It Gives Me a Headache.

Steve Gottlieb
Founder and CEO, Shindig

I GRADUATED HARVARD LAW SCHOOL WITH ONLY one clear career decision: to avoid becoming a lawyer at all costs. As is customary, the year before graduation I summered at a law firm. While the generous salaries, lavish meals, and other incentives were intended to impress upon recruits how wonderful life as a partner might be, they did little to overcome the queasiness I felt from my first day in the office. Devoid of the big picture of business motivations, the piecework that comprised summer associates' day-to-day labor seemed incredibly mechanical and uninteresting. More significantly, it did not seem any more appealing further up the ranks. I didn't want to be part of an assembly line, whether it was turning out metal stampings or legal filings.

To ensure I would never fall back into the clutches of a cushy legal job, I grew my hair long. By the time firms were on campus the following spring making final hiring decisions, my appearance had become entirely Wall Street inappropriate.

Non-interest in law school thankfully left me with plenty of time to cook up business plans. I'd left law school briefly after my first year with a plan to start a cable business news channel, but having been unable to find backing, I returned at the end of summer for my second year. Fax technology was just coming out in 1984. At $20,000 per machine, it was still a long way from becoming part of standard office equipment, let alone a staple of consumer electronics. FedEx were the pioneers in popularizing fax usage with a service they called Zap mail. I had a plan for a low-cost competitor super-serving the finance industry with locations only in the top ten markets.

Several other promising plans were put together on my hand-me-down Selectric, with accompanying spreadsheets created on a Hewlett Packard 110 with Lotus123 version 1A. Among the competitors for my attention was an idea that a buddy had brought to me. He loved old TV themes. He would sit at the piano and play them, one after another, for friends. He'd had the idea of somehow capturing that experience on a record but was not sure how to go about it.

With a handful of business plans in tow I began meeting entrepreneurs and successful business people, searching for advice on what to do with my life. Though I sought a meeting with Alan R. Trustman, my knowledge of him was limited. This was pre-Internet; one took meetings with the barest of real information on people. He was the dad of a smart and idiosyncratic friend from school, John Trustman. John himself had cut quite a figure. During college, he had spent much time and money restoring an old Maserati—an unusual activity for an undergraduate at Yale! His past seemed filled with exotic stories.

Consistent with John's allure, his father was, among other things, held out as a fabulously wealthy eccentric. He had been the highest paid screenwriter in Hollywood, having written *The Thomas Crown Affair, Bullitt,* and who knew what else. He was purportedly part-owner of a hot audio-video equipment company, Advent, at a time when stereo companies (especially those making the new room-size projection TVs) were the definition of hi tech.

The lunch was no-nonsense. *What did I want? How could he help?* Like every naive person starting out, I somehow always hoped that grownup business people would actually be interested in helping me figure out the answers to the big questions like *what to do with my life.* I told him I was looking for advice, that I understood him to be a successful entrepreneur, and perhaps he could tell me which of the things I was working on offered the most promise, in his opinion.

I went through my pitch for the collection of TV themes. People loved TV themes. Many had been hits, and the music was wonderful. (Lalo Schifrin, who had done *Mission: Impossible,* had previously scored *Bullitt*). I'd grown up helping a family business whose first products were pop art replicas of commercial products: blow-up Chiquita bananas and Campbell Soup garbage cans. They became a popular fad of the early '70s. My instincts told me that there was inherent irresistible love for reproductions of the familiar ignored touchstones of pop culture—and that a loving collection of TV themes would, in the same fashion, be a hit.

This took a bit of a leap. *Trivial Pursuit* had been a success, but 1984 was still early in the rediscovery and re-appreciation of TV culture that was about to occur. It was before *Star Trek: Next Generation,* let alone *Deep Space Nine, Voyager,* or *Enterprise*; before Broadway productions of the *Addams Family,* let alone *Gilligan's Island, The Musical*; before live action features of everything from *The Flintstones* to *George of the Jungle 2*; before knowing the names of the *Brady Bunch* cast members was considered anything other than especially odd.

Alan was initially puzzled. "Don't such things already exist?"

"Well, yes," I explained, "but only as souvenirs. Releases issued for 'fanatics,' or opportunistic collections done by one studio or record company to exploit rights they held for a small group of themes. They'd have been compiled based somewhat arbitrarily either on which studio had an interest in the show the theme came from, or which record company represented the composer or performer for multiple themes. No one's ever done an overview of TV themes as a genre. Moreover, no one's approached the short original themes as a pop culture phenomenon in and of themselves. Because pop songs are expected to be three to five minutes in length, not thirty to sixty seconds, the original TV themes have always been understood as not good enough to stand on their own; to do that, they would need to be expanded into five-minute suites. My idea is to assemble the original short versions."

"So how would you go about it?"

"Well, not only would we have to get a license from each composer's representative, their music publishers, who might control a portion of the song rights, but we'd have to go back to each of the original production companies that likely owned the underlying rights to a show's theme recordings—a different set of rights. There are potentially hundreds, and the rights have changed hands frequently over the years as a company's uneven successes have led to merger, acquisition, maybe disintegration. I would have to not only track down all these companies, then convince them it is in their interest to do a deal in which—precisely because each theme is so short, and the project involves several hundred royalty participants—each company's individual share would be a tiny fraction, and the advance available to them, even presuming some success, would not cover much in the way of legal and administrative fees required to dig through files that might not have been touched in decades."

Alan looked up, smiled, then made a face. I'd had him for a minute, it seemed. "Great idea, but *it gives me a headache.* What else?"

That was it. Our conversation moved on to other projects, but his comment would resonate for years to come and return at many of my most critical moments of decision. And it was those words—it gives me a headache—that inspired me to move forward.

What, after all, did I have to offer the world at twenty-seven? What was my special "value add" that would possibly justify people compensating me? Here was a project that for all intents and purposes seemed to have great potential. But its sole drawback was that it required the willingness for someone to deal with a mountain of problems ... it was going to give someone a big headache.

For me the phrase encapsulated what a business opportunity was. What the act of creation indeed was. *The willingness to do work.* To commit effort, energy, whatever it took. To do something acknowledged as possibly a good idea, but for which the principal reason it had not been done previously was that in order to achieve it, the job would be messy, or time-consuming, or difficult. Not insurmountable, just a pain. And the kind of pain that typically kept away normal people who were not desperate to create something new, or not sufficiently passionate, or not convinced about the worth of the effort.

For me, willingness to have a headache that no one else was willing to have became my business mantra. So after *Television's Greatest Hits* blossomed into its own pop phenomena, I faced a host of other decisions that were informed by that construct. Why did independent record companies invariably do distribution deals with major labels? Why not distribute directly to retailers? Wasn't that relationship obviously critical to the success of a record at retail? But it was a headache that required a focus on sell-through and long-term marketing, so TVT Records became unique in having its own distribution system and a complementary creative approach. Why take on breaking artists through grassroots marketing to thousands of small outlets and with specially organized street teams, when it seemed easier just to go to the much smaller number of power brokers at Top 40 radio? That sounded like a headache; but, as it turned out, a headache worth having. TVT earned its expertise in developing grassroots successes from Nine Inch Nails to Pitbull.

And now, many years after, in my latest venture, Shindig, I'm trying to create a wholly new online social experience with large-scale video chat events. We are in effect competing with video chat offerings from Google, Skype, Apple, and other tech giants—trying to innovate upon a video chat experience that has really not been reimagined since first attempted fifty years ago at the '64 World's Fair as the Picturephone. It is the willingness to build something from the ground up, and have a headache that others would not typically choose to undertake, that informs the effort.

Each case meant coming up with an answer for myself as to why I was so lucky to be staring at a business opportunity previously out there for all to see. *What impediment blinded others to the opportunity?* was the question that needed a satisfactory answer before committing myself. Having a headache became a key to distinguishing bad ideas from good.

An instance where clearing an obstacle was too expensive to justify or impossible for some other reason: those were bad ideas, no matter the access to funding or seeming good prospects. Something where the principal reason for not occurring was the fact that no one had previously been willing to undertake the challenge—those instances where it just seemed like too much or too complicated or too messy a job—those seemed to be the good ideas. Those opportunities, provided the blinkered view that led others to choose not to do it could be identified, were potentially the good ideas, ideas where the value add I could provide seemed clearly justifiable and sustainable.

Choosing to have a headache was not perhaps the least stressful choice to make. But it has certainly led to an interesting career.

DOING WELL
=== AND ===
DOING GOOD

Doing Well and Doing Good.

Jens Molbak
Founder and CEO, Coinstar

WHERE DO STARTUP IDEAS COME FROM? I WAS AS
surprised as anyone that my idea manifested itself in a mason jar full
of coins on my dresser top. Since the time I founded Coinstar when
I was twenty-six, the network of kiosks has recycled over one trillion
coins, worth over $40 billion, and donated $80 million to charities.

I've spoken in many classrooms and to many aspiring entrepreneurs and am most often asked two questions:

⇨ *How did you come up with the idea of counting pennies
for a startup?*

⇨ *How can new entrepreneurs come up with their own
innovative ideas?*

I'll start with the second question and then return to the first.

Want to find a cool idea for a new startup that can grow into
something substantial? Look to the public sector. Yes, that's right,
to *government.* I believe that new startups can thrive where there are
inefficiencies in the market, and the government offers many opportunities. Pick any federal or state organization and ask if there

125

is a way for the private sector to help provide better service(s). Do research, brainstorm, and see what you find.

That's part of what I did when I created Coinstar. Like many of my college friends, I hoped for a career that would enable me to do well for myself and my future family, and to do good for society. Many of us envisioned first working in the private sector, then shifting more focus to the nonprofit and public sectors as our careers advanced. But I wanted to impact all three sectors simultaneously. The problem was I couldn't find a job that enabled me to have such an impact, so I was left to create my own. And if it worked, I'd be able to hire my friends who also wanted to do well and do good. A win/win all around.

But what did that job look like? Back to the mason jar. As a kid, my bank used to count my loose coins for me, but then they stopped and gave me a bunch of paper wrappers. Being lazy, I wanted a machine to do it for me. After doing research with the U. S. Mint and consumers, I realized there were $8 billion of coins in America's collective mason jars, and that $150 billion flowed through consumer hands annually. That was a big enough private sector market to start a company. I also realized that if it worked, Coinstar would become the national coin recycling program, lessening the U. S. Mint's needs to spend money and produce unnecessary coins. I estimated the public sector savings to be $200 million annually.

Research also showed the long history of coins and charity: March of Dimes, Salvation Army's red buckets, Unicef's orange Halloween boxes. So I decided to give consumers the choice of converting their loose coins back into cash or donating to a charity of their choice.

My coin jar led to the creation of a company that could win in the private sector, while simultaneously benefiting the public and nonprofit sectors. This was my first chance to integrate doing well and doing good.

I believe there are hundreds of more opportunities like this. Go get 'em ... and let me know how I can help!

Watch the Parking Meters.

Steve Tomlin
General Partner, Avalon Ventures
Serial Entrepreneur

"Don't follow leaders/Watch the parkin'meters"
~Bob Dylan, "Subterranean Homesick Blues"

IF YOU REALLY WANT TO BE AN ENTREPRENEUR, AND you will know if you do (because you can't possibly imagine yourself wanting a "real job"), you must expand your realms of knowledge, hang out with odd people, and not settle into any comfortable job for very long right out of college or grad school. Beware of the prestigious and lucrative post-education job offer, because you will adapt your lifestyle to your excessive compensation; then pretty soon it won't seem excessive, and you will crave promotions and a bigger salary. You will wake up one day and realize that you've signed a Faustian, or perhaps Dilbertian, deal.

"But wait," you say. "If I give some time to The Man, I will then have *savings*, a Scrooge McDuck-like money pile earned from my career at Smartypants-For-Hire, Inc. or the prestigious firm of Salitieri, Poore, Nash, De Brutus and Short. With that financial safety net, not to mention my worldly wisdom and my social network, I will *then* pursue my entrepreneurial career while still living in stately Wayne Manor."

Ummmm ... no.

Right now you have a huge *advantage* being young and naive, well-*un*connected to anyone of power or importance, capable of wandering freely and living cheaply, unafraid to ask dumb questions and pursue odd interests and lucid dreams. Don't sell out and squander these powers. Pursued early in your career, your entrepreneurial risks are nearly free, unencumbered by expectation or "opportunity cost." But, after your three-piece kryptonite suit at PrestigeCo, you won't be faster than a speeding bullet. "It's a bird, it's a plane, it's ... oh, never mind, it's a bird." Yep, you'll be just another bird.

So do the following:

Take plenty of humanities courses so you will learn to think deeply and communicate thoughtfully, but also join Yale's CEID (Center for Engineering Innovation and Design) to become a "maker-geek," getting your hands dirty crafting prototypes and designing clever devices. Play at the interstices of disciplines, find the edges and seek overlap. Talk to people who are discussing things you don't understand.

Take an astronomy course. The sooner you realize that you're essentially pointless in the grand scheme of things, the better. And, armed with a sense of your own cosmic worthlessness, you will be less likely to take yourself too seriously or accept the self-important rubbish that GreyFlannel Ltd. is peddling.

Take a philosophy course, especially one that covers ethics. Given the irrepressible march of technology into every arena of life, including into life itself, the biggest issues you may face as an entrepreneur could be pretty deep ones: so be armed.

Learn to write well. Entrepreneurs need to explain their ideas;

they are assumed to be insane unless they can talk and present their way into convincing people otherwise (or, for that matter, how about taking a drama class or joining a production?).

If you're not one yourself, have a few decent software programmers within your circle of friends. Trust me on this; someday one of them will help you.

Hang out at YEI (Yale Entrepreneurial Institute) to see what it really means to launch a startup, i.e., not for weak-kneed dilettantes. Maybe even apply to one of their periodic student venture competitions.

Now, the last and most important suggestion:

Network "weirdly," e.g., find out what a Yale School of Forestry and Environmental Science grad student is working on (did you even know that Yale *had* a forestry school?); talk to students and faculty working on matters involving "Big Data;" meet someone at Yale's Divinity School and try to imagine what an entrepreneur could possibly work on there; sneak into a faculty symposium (preferably a technical one), sit in the back row and try to understand what they're talking about (for extra credit, raise your hand and ask a question); buttonhole alumni to learn what they do and whether or not they're happy doing it, and ask them to tell you how they ended up where they are; spend a few months in China; read a pile of trade magazines from an industry that interests you; go to TEDx events, or at least watch a bunch of TEDx videos; phone (don't email) ten important Yale alums in a field that interests you and pitch them your crazy entrepreneurial idea—you'll be amazed at how many will take your call. Maybe some will even help you.

Well, I think you get the idea. Stay light, move fast, think deeply and widely, network weirdly. Don't follow leaders (but do listen to them and attend their lectures), and watch the parking meters (so you don' get stuck too long in one place).

Difference Between Business Development and Sales.

Victor Wong
CEO, PaperG

A COMMON AND UNDERSTANDABLE QUESTION THAT comes up a lot in business and startups is, "What's the difference between business development and sales?" Knowing the difference is important for how you approach hiring, growing, and ultimately succeeding, as I came to found out.

WHAT PEOPLE THINK THE DIFFERENCE IS

MBAs love applying for jobs with "business development" in the title, but they rarely take on positions for sales. Is it simply the same job but with a far more impressive-sounding title? Is it perhaps similar but involves "strategic thinking" along with "business development?"

The confusion stems from the fact that many companies use the terms interchangeably, when the two are actually quite different. While the stereotypes of each role don't capture the nuances of the differences, they do illustrate them quite well. Most people imagine that business development is taking a lot of meetings over coffee and drinks where you talk about how you should be working together. Many people imagine sales to be either door-to-door or over-the-phone high pressure selling.

While these images help explain what most business development and sales people spend their time doing, it doesn't quite explain how the end results are different, because in both cases, the client or customer is choosing to work with you in the end.

WHAT THE DIFFERENCE IS

The difference is simply this: in business development, you're convincing people to make a decision they don't have to make, while in sales, you're convincing people to make a decision they have to make.

Business development is convincing companies to partner with your company or to do something they don't have to do, yet it's something that would likely be mutually beneficial. Examples would be companies distributing/selling your product, promoting you, or referring customers to you (or vice versa). In effect, all these benefits are nice to have, but they are not core to the existing strategy of the target partner. All of these could, in fact, be gigantic wastes of time and resources.

As a business development professional, you're supposed to convince people to ignore the downsides and focus on the upsides of partnership, while also adding urgency for the person to do it now. Business development can create enormous leverage in value for a business by generating whole new channels for reaching customers rather than just optimizing a single existing channel. Oftentimes, business development professionals only deal with other business development professionals or senior executives who handle conversations with other companies.

In contrast, sales people normally are selling to the end users who need your product to do their job or a procurement officer in charge of buying certain things that people in the company absolutely need to have to do their job. In these cases, the decision maker typically has a lot of choices. So the job of the sales person is to convince the decision maker that one product is better than another. There's typically a self-imposed timeline due to the urgency of upgrading or getting ahold of a product to help with core business operations. The value of sales beyond generating revenue is talking to the end customers and gaining valuable feedback to incorporate into the product, which you don't really get clearly from a business development partner.

I'm not sure I can say definitively which of the two jobs is harder, because it depends entirely on an individual's skillset and personality. Business development does require strategic thinking—so you can explain why it makes sense for both companies to change their product or distribution roadmap. Sales requires some user-experience thinking in order to explain why a product is best designed for a particular user. They both require skills of persuasion.

That said, I do think business development is incredibly difficult from a time standpoint. It's hard to create urgency when there isn't any; in addition, it's hard to measure whether someone makes progress or success in business development. Consequently, business development may be ultimately harder to succeed in, because it requires a lot of faith and time. But if you can convince someone to do something they don't have to do, you have a really valuable skill.

Either way, it does still boil down to: deal or no deal?

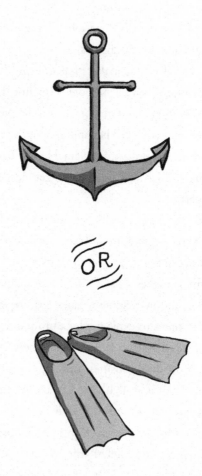

Sink or Swim.

Julia Pimsleur
Founder and CEO, Little Pim
Blogger of "Language Learning for Kids," Forbes

I WAS NO DIFFERENT THAN ANY OTHER SIX-YEAR-old girl when I walked into class on my first day of first grade. Except the teacher spoke only French, the kids were all French, and I was the only American.

My father, Dr. Paul Pimsleur, who created the groundbreaking Pimsleur Method®, had moved our family to Paris, France, and I and my brother were enrolled in a French public school. Within three months, we became perfectly bilingual. This early immersion experience changed my life forever. I always felt that teaching me to speak French was the greatest gift my parents ever gave me—it opened doors for me culturally, educationally, and professionally. And I don't even remember learning. Years later, it was this ease of learning that I sought out to recreate for my own sons when I came up with Little Pim, an at-home immersion language teaching method designed to introduce young kids to a second or third language before the age of six.

I set out to change the way children learn languages. As a mother, filmmaker, and daughter of a language-teaching pioneer, I felt uniquely motivated and qualified to create the first method specifically designed for young children. I spent two years creating the Entertainment Immersion Method®, working with a leading neuroscientist, educators, and language experts. I launched my company with my savings and funds raised from friends and family. The series teaches 360 words and phrases and makes language-learning easy for kids and simple for parents, even if they don't speak the language themselves. Little Pim has since sold over two million products and offers twelve languages, including Chinese, Arabic, and Russian.

Whether you're learning a new language or starting your own company, it's crucial to have faith in yourself. The odds are against you, and any hesitation will not help your cause. Believe in yourself, jump in, and you will come out the other side a stronger person. It's all up to you.

Connect Your Passion to Helping Others.

Marc A. Perry
Founder and CEO, BuiltLean

WHEN I WAS A SENIOR AT YALE, I DECIDED TO FOL-
low the herd into finance. I thought that after getting some analytical
and accounting experience, I could leave to start my own business
within a couple of years.

After five years of sitting in front of a computer in finance doing something I wasn't passionate about, I finally had the courage to
leave. It was one of the best decisions of my life. The pull of a corporate job is so strong that it can be very difficult to consider a life
outside of it. Also, leaving to start a business may seem like financial
suicide, which makes it even harder to leave.

I urge you to analyze yourself and think about the things you
love to do. My opinion is that you can do anything you want to do
and create whatever life or career you want. If you know who you are
and what you want, it makes life a lot easier. As Lao-Tsu proclaimed
over a thousand years ago, "He who conquers others is strong; he
who conquers himself is mighty."

I encourage you to answer these two questions:

⇨ *What would I do if I could not fail?* There are no limits—you will succeed at whatever you decide to do. If there is no fear of failure, what would you do?

⇨ *What is my true purpose in life?* Spend fifteen minutes writing down everything that comes to mind.

Answering these two questions changed my life. I soon created a career mission to help busy people improve their fitness in less time and with less hassle. While I didn't have a big business idea, I knew this mission is something that I could pursue for the rest of my life. It wasn't an easy transition to become an entrepreneur and fulfill my mission, but it was worth it in spades. *I believe that if you connect your passion to helping other people, then you are onto something that can make you genuinely happy.*

The most common reason I hear for why people don't do something entrepreneurial is they don't have a business idea. My answer—be proactive. Create a mission. What is your mission in *your* life? Then consider all the problems you face every day.

Business idea generation is not passive, but a very active endeavor. Come up with a few ideas every day, if that's your stumbling block. As you learn more about your mission, you will likely come across business ideas along the way. For example, I knew I wanted to figure out a way to help busy professionals get in better shape in less time and with less hassle, so I just started working toward that mission. That mission evolved into a business I started that now has customers in over one hundred countries. I'm also a fitness coach and trainer with my own YouTube channel, which I never could have imagined happening when I was in finance!

I hope you have the courage to think differently, follow your passion, and work very hard connecting your passion to helping other people. I think it's a recipe for much happiness and success.

A Dose of Pragmatism.

Sheldon Gilbert
Founder and CEO, Proclivity Media

FAR TOO OFTEN PEOPLE PURSUE THE TREACHEROUS and often rewarding path of being an entrepreneur as a result of superficial commercialistic notions of astronomical wealth being created in just a couple of years and instant celebrity status being achieved. Aspiring entrepreneurs should disabuse themselves of these notions for two reasons: one, these are incredibly rare cases that occur often due more to transient market hyperboles than viable business models; and two, these are insipid personal motivations that do not provide the "intestinal fortitude" required to truly succeed.

Visionaries are ones who often see a solution when others are blinded by seemingly intractable barriers, and entrepreneurs are the deeply impassioned individuals who are crazy enough to execute on the vision despite overwhelming doubt and cynicism. What compels the often successful entrepreneur isn't narcissism or being a contrarian, but rather one who is convinced that there is a more elegant, efficient, and productive solution to a fundamental problem. One has to be incorrigibly obsessed with the singular pursuit of the better solution for others. Otherwise it will become incredibly difficult to withstand and survive the natural vicissitudes of launching a new company with limited capital, well-financed incumbents, new competitors, personal setbacks, delayed product launches, product defects, exasperated clients, limited sleep, overworked staff, and a now-cold tomato soup that you forgot to eat since that sales call eight hours earlier.

Given all of this, my one piece of advice, which has served me well as a first-time entrepreneur and allowed me to appreciate various successes and navigate several failures and multiple mistakes, is to make sure you are solving a real problem that has an addressable market. It is imperative that you understand the value chain of your industry and where you exist within that value chain. If you haven't given this some thought and are not aware of whom you may or may not be displacing or whether you are creating an entirely new value chain altogether, which requires change in behavior of your target market, then you need to stop now and find your North Star. It will help guide nearly all of your decisions as to who to hire, in which city to set up shop, which investors to choose, terms by which you'll raise capital, your revenue model, your operational model, how you'll scale, potential partners, awareness of the true competitors, and how to obviate their challenges, your potential exit strategies, etc.

The notion of "building it first and the market will come" or "first mover advantage" can be dangerous strategies to pursue, given that the cost of entering the market and starting a company has gone down considerably, particularly in the Internet and software technology sectors, as the cost of storage and processing are a fraction of what they were a decade ago and access to early-stage capital is at an all-time high. You are much better served understanding the fundamental issue that you are solving—which, by the way, isn't usually subject to dramatic change over short periods of time—and utilize a limited amount of capital to rapidly develop and market test the idea with an initial set of beta clients to truly understand the benefits and limitations of your solution and have the ability to rapidly adjust and modify your solution to truly meet the market needs.

Those companies without their North Star end up being victims of change and constantly flip their business focus, only to go out of business, versus those who have a clear understanding of the fundamental problem they are solving and become the change agents and adjust and refine along the way to allow them to get closer to the optimal solution.

Consider this a dose of pragmatism in a world often saturated with hyperbole. Make sure you are solving a real problem and make sure you are not the only one who thinks that this is a problem.

May the force be with you.

Work with What and Who You Love.

Tom Lehman and Ilan Zechory
Founders, Genius

OVER THE LAST SIX YEARS, GENIUS HAS EVOLVED from a fun little project among friends to a global community of more than thirty million scholars with a collective mission to annotate the world. It's been crazy to experience so much change. What started as a place to decode rap lyrics has become a platform to break down literature and screenplays, legal texts, historical speeches, and on and on.

Our goal—and one of the keys to our success—has been to think of ourselves not as entrepreneurs, but rather as friends working really hard on an art project. We're die-hard rap fans, so we built a community around that. We didn't intend for this to become a business at first. It was a passion project based on the things we were already interested in—hip-hop, the arts, and sharing knowledge among intellectually curious people. As the interests of the community expanded, the project expanded along with them.

The most successful ventures are not ones where someone sets out to make a lot of money, but where someone looks at what they're passionate about and says, "*How can I work with people who care about the things I care about? How can I kick-start a real community, and then earnestly participate in it alongside everyone else?*"

BUILDING SOMETHING takes a CERTAIN AMOUNT of GRUBBY AMBITION

Hate to Be Him.

Rob Long
Television Writer and Producer

LET ME ASK YOU A QUESTION. IF SOMEONE GAVE YOU, say, fifty million dollars today, would you think that's a lot of money? I'm not ashamed to say that personally speaking, I would. But yesterday, I was lunching in a local establishment and overheard two guys in t-shirts talking about a recent big screen release.

"Yeah, you know, it kinda bombed, man," one of them said with a sort of sad, slightly disparaging tone of voice. "I mean, it only made, like, fifty million dollars."

The other dude nodded sadly. "Fifty million!" he scoffed. "How embarrassing! That guy's career is, like, dead."

"Hate to be him," said the other one.

"Guys," I said, interrupting their conversation. "Can I get my turkey sandwich?"

You see, I was at a local sandwich shop, and the two guys—with such lofty and inflexible standards about what, exactly, constitutes success in the entertainment business—were behind the counter, stuffing pita bread and slicing turkey for what I'm guessing was roughly nine dollars an hour.

And it struck me that this kind of thing happens a lot in Hollywood and, probably, in places where there are lots of dreamy young people with towering expectations of entitlement—people scoffing at what are actually large sums of money, just because they're not *huge* sums of money. People calling something a failure just because the sky didn't open up and rain lucre on everyone involved in the show or the movie. Of course, it's one thing to have this attitude from the deck of your beach house in Malibu—if you've ever had a hit, you're qualified to judge. But it's quite another to be in your twenties looking down your nose at something when your hands are spreading mayonnaise and mustard on my turkey sandwich.

Years ago, when I was a young screenwriter, I found myself at lunch with a few older producers. They were all funny, cynical guys—nice to me, but sharp and competitive with each other. And each one of them had a number of giant hits to his credit.

At one point during lunch, I made a passing, dismissive remark about one of the most famous movie flops of all time, *Howard the Duck*. I can't remember what, exactly, I said, but it was in the same vein as my sandwich dudes. Something along the lines of, "Boy, I'd hate to be the guy who did that movie."

The conversation stopped. The producers, who up to that moment had been sparring and jabbing each other, looked at me with incredulity.

Finally, one of them spoke up.

"What are you talking about? That movie made millions. Don't say stupid things, kid. Make a movie yourself. Make a *hit* movie yourself. Then, maybe, you can derogate."

My face got hot and red with shame. I sputtered my apologies. They all smiled and shrugged. And one of them added, "Don't worry about it, kiddo. You'll learn. The thing is, the trick to moviemaking is to make money no matter what. Even on a flop, to use your word. I made a movie once that cost thirty-six million dollars. It made eight million back. Technically, the movie lost twenty-eight million dollars."

His eyes suddenly twinkled. "But somehow," he said, with a huge grin, "I ended up making six million. Do you get it?"

I didn't, really. And still don't, unfortunately. But I'm trying.

And that's my advice for entrepreneurs coming out of a fancy school: it's almost impossible not to shake your reflexive snobbery, your hard-won expectation that everything you touch will be gilded and glamorous.

But building something—whether a television show, a business, or an iPhone app—takes a certain amount of grubby ambition. It takes humility. It takes a willingness to do something that sounds unfancy and unglamorous and risk the most status-killing thing of them all: failure.

In any endeavor, it's not failure you should fear. It's snobbery.

Fall in Love with a Problem.

Sandeep Ayyappan
Founder and CEO, Delve

IT OVERCOMES YOU. A SENSE OF FRUSTRATION SO deep that it makes you cast aside whatever your goal was so you can find a solution. One so aggravating that it makes you go through the misery of creating your own flawed method to alleviate the root cause. Every so often in life, each of us encounters it. Most of us simply let those moments pass with a sigh of exasperation and a look to the heavens, but occasionally those moments are a spark of creativity.

Problems are everywhere. The really big ones aren't easy to solve, nor are solutions obvious. In Startupland, most prefer to talk about the solution—the company, the startup, the process, raising capital, building a team, and whatnot—but let's look a bit harder at what happens long before any of that.

What are problems? It's easiest to think about problems by looking at a couple of the most obvious.

Communicating with other people has been a constant source of struggle for us. A number of issues are troublesome: you may not know where the other person is, or how to reach them, or when to reach them, or even who you want to reach. They may or may not be interested in your message. Your message may not reach them. We've invented lots of ideas to help with this, dating a long way back—paper and pen, the telegraph, the telephone, email. Our tools these days are so efficient that the problem has evolved—instead of not being able to send people messages, many people are now overwhelmed by the number of emails they receive.

Here's another: even the speediest and toughest of us can't move as quickly as we'd like to on our own. Since the invention of the wheel, we've worked hard to build tools that help us move ourselves and our things. As those tools became more powerful—railways, automobiles, planes—society has become more dispersed and yet more interconnected.

When we think about examples such as these, we can see a few patterns emerge. The first is that the biggest problems aren't limited to a particular medium—their scale is simply at the level of humanity. Until we can read each other's minds, we'll always be working to improve our interpersonal communication. Email has made it simpler to send a note than snail mail, and the telephone made the messenger unnecessary, but we still have plenty of times when a message doesn't get to its intended recipient. Whether the medium is a rock, paper, or a kilobyte, it still takes plenty of things to go exactly right for an effective transfer of ideas to occur.

Another pattern worth noting is that the nature of a problem evolves dramatically over time. If you were flying in the 1960s, you probably never saw another plane in the air. Yet today, flights in the crowded northeast fly well out into the Atlantic to alleviate air traffic. The idea that we'd be tight on airspace would probably be inconceivable to someone decades ago, yet today planes waste tons of fuel and plenty of their passengers' time circling airports or taking wide diversions just to avoid other planes. Right now, we're living through a fundamental shift in the way our automotive industry powers itself, and it's very possible that kids growing up two decades from now might only see internal combustion engines in museums. What problems might this create? How will we generate all of the additional electricity required to power millions of vehicles? How do we recycle our huge volumes of batteries? Some of these could well become the problems our kids spend their careers solving.

The problem I love: I sat at a wooden table on the front porch of a comfortable house in Abilene, Texas. It was a warm spring night in April of 2010, and I'd just started a long road trip gathering perspectives on the energy industry. Around me were three oil guys—a landman, a rig operator, and a guy who owned a handful of drilling sites. We went through beers and stories, my recorder capturing tales of getting shot at after going through the wrong fence, of piles of money thrown at wells that never performed. Finally, we got to a deep conversation about the role of regulation in oil drilling. I heard over and over about the number of regulations they had to deal with—environmental reporting and safety precautions, processes around cleaning up the site and disposing of water. I asked why these were in place, how foolproof the process was these days, and what the chances might be for a big oil well blowout. Not possible, I was told.

Within a week, oil began gushing from the Macondo well in the Gulf of Mexico as the Deepwater Horizon blew up and sank.

The amount of information we have at our fingertips has never been greater in human history. Technology has dramatically changed how much of it there is and how quickly we can access it. Decisions these days are made on the basis of more research and data than ever before, and finger-in-the-wind intuition has been marginalized and proven false repeatedly. Yet those of us who should be best prepared and most knowledgeable on certain topics fall well short of making the right decision much of the time.

Here's one where perfect will never be achievable—it's very difficult (and often impossible) to even define what the perfect decision is in most situations. But we can work towards it by surrounding ourselves with the best possible information, by building tools that help us retain it as knowledge, and ultimately grow wiser as individuals, as leaders, and as a society. How can we do it?

We need to create immensely more amounts of raw data, and then we need ridiculous amounts of computing power to make it usable. We then need armies of researchers to find patterns in it and to extrapolate valuable conclusions from it. We need to make all of this information searchable and easy to discuss, and then we need a bunch of brilliant communicators to bring this information into our schools, our companies, our government, our societies—journalists and professors, teachers and bloggers. And then it's up to the rest of us to soak it all in, to ingest it and remember it, and then to apply it to situations where it helps us pick the right path.

This is a fundamental struggle of humanity, and there are massive inefficiencies at every step. When I was a senior sociology major at Yale, I did a study on high school students around New Haven for my senior thesis. I surveyed students at a few different schools and gathered some data on how their professional ambitions evolved between their freshman and senior years. What I found wasn't surprising, but it affected me deeply: freshmen at the schools I studied were similarly ambitious, but seniors at schools where they had more exposure to professionals, more mentorship, and better information about careers maintained their levels of ambition much more so than students at schools where there was less of it.

Knowledge empowers us. Yet we have large strides to make in identifying and distributing quality information and building knowledge. Technology has enabled a fleet of solutions to emerge—from free access anywhere to Wikipedia to Google's ability to find a limitless amount of information to my Weather app—but there's plenty of situations in which we have little or no data, and plenty where we can't tell the difference between good and bad information, and plenty more where one of us knows the answer, but we can't get that knowledge to someone who could have used it. I love being able to work on this problem every day.

The Missouri River runs along the east side of Omaha, Nebraska, where I grew up. Towards the northeast of the city lies Carter Lake, a horseshoe shaped body of water near Eppley Airfield, Omaha's humble, charming airport. But this lake wasn't always a lake—it used to be a bend in the Missouri. Over centuries, the river kept running into its walls as it rushed around a corner until it slowly carved a more direct route along the track it currently owns. Sediment piled up along the longer track until it was completely cut off from the Missouri (lakes like these are called oxbow lakes).

Somewhere along that process, there was a single molecule of water that was foolish enough to think there might be a better way towards the Gulf. And then came another, and another, and a whole bunch more until they carved a new path downstream. Creating better pathways, it seems, couldn't be more natural.

The path that each of us is on will hardly ever be a straight one. There will be twists, turns, and a constant series of problems. Each of these is an opportunity for a new way to do something and potentially the foundation for a great company. Keep a close eye on every single one—it just may be your real way forward.

Passion Above All.

Kevin Lee
CEO, Didit
CEO, We-Care.com

FOLLOW YOUR PASSION. DON'T JUST DECIDE YOU want to start a business and start looking around for a business to build. Anyone can look online through the franchise pages in *Inc. Magazine*. The real fun lies in having the epiphany that there is a problem out there that you can solve and for which you think people will pay to have the solution.

My first business was as an undergrad. While it was nothing fancy (combining food delivery from three restaurants), it met a need, and I figured it would be fun and lucrative. It was. My second startup was a digital media agency in 1994, and my current firm is essentially a spinoff of that agency.

I loved the area of search engine marketing and decided to focus on that specific area of digital marketing. A logical expansion was when the engines started auctioning off clicks participating in those marketplaces, as was the evolution into auction-based social media clicks and auction-based display media. All of that is really fun for an economics undergrad with an MBA from Yale who loves marketing and advertising.

Sure, I could have taken a different route, working for an investment bank out of grad school or even becoming one of Google's first hundred employees (that might have been a more lucrative decision), but instead I stuck with doing what I love and was able to also launch a social entrepreneurship venture on the side, helping nonprofits tap the power of cause marketing with We-Care.com.

As an aside, one other important tip is "don't underestimate the importance of good HR/staff." Almost every business wins by execution, not by the idea. For that, you need great people.

PEOPLE.

It Really Is the People.

David Meyers, Ph.D.
Principal, Green Ant Advisors

THERE IS ONE THREAD THAT KEEPS RETURNING TO my entrepreneurial experiences, which I wish I had really understood at the start. Everyone will tell you that it's about "people, people, people" and you say, "Yes, of course it's about people," just as I did. However, here is my little hint: It *really is* about people.

I have started and been part of the early stages of five companies. None have been huge financial successes, but all had great value to me in terms of learning about different businesses—from the Internet in the late 1990s through "triple bottom line" investing more recently. In each case, the people involved did "make or break" the startup. So a few hard lessons learned along the way:

#1 TRUST YOUR GUT.

People can be very deceptive, and often our entrepreneurial enthusiasm can push us to accept situations that are not ideal. We may hope that at some point—when such-and-such happens—it will work out. When you feel deep in your gut that someone is going to be a problem, share that with a mentor, and get a second or third opinion. Speak up about it. Startups are too small, and everyone has to pull their weight. Bad apples in a large company might be manageable. Bad apples in a startup are disastrous.

#2 DON'T WAIT.

When you sense a problem with a partner or co-founder, or top exec, address it right away. There are too many things to continuously do in a startup, and if something is put off for the future, it becomes difficult to get back to. Patterns are set quickly.

If there is a problem, address it immediately and address it completely. If you can't work out an effective solution, get out. I have done that twice now and am extremely grateful that I moved when I did. We pour too much money and heart into our companies, so don't wait around thinking things might get better. If there is a problem, address it, and if that fails—walk away.

#3 BUILD THE RIGHT TEAM.

Companies are, by definition, groups of people and teams. Don't stop searching for great people to be part of your team. Be extremely choosy about who joins you. Do not accept anyone who is willing to work for equity—even interns require time, attention, and will have an impact on the culture of an early-stage company.

There are amazing people out there, and many of the best will be completely different from you. Do not only seek people who are the same. Diversity is key. One effective way to assure good "people choices" is to make sure every choice is agreed upon by at least three people who assess the individual as independently as possible.

#4 AVOID HIERARCHICAL PEOPLE.

When it's all about position, it's not about the company. Infighting is such a distraction that it leads to bad decision-making.

#5 FINALLY, HAVE FUN.

If you are not having fun, something is wrong that needs fixing. Entrepreneurship is not easy, but enjoying it means you are on the right track.

Yes, Your People Is the Secret.

Ingrid Stabb

Author, *The Career Within You*

Named Among the Top 100 Most Desired Mentors for Gen-Y

IN MY SECOND ENTREPRENEURIAL VENTURE AFTER college, I was one of three founding team members of Score! Learning Corporation, a for-profit chain located in shopping centers. Parents could drop off their kids to brush up on math, reading, and science on computers, while the children also had fun earning kudos and prizes.

In the beginning, the three of us ran only one learning center next to an ice cream store in Palo Alto, California. But we had a big dream. Envisioning a national chain of computer learning centers, when the phone rang, one of us would swish across the store in our nylon coach's uniform and answer the phone, "Hello, Score! Advantage Centers." Emphasis on the plural "s."

It was hard work to hone our business model and hustle to bring in and retain enough customers to keep this first center open and start expanding to centers #2 and #3. Sure enough, within a few years we had opened 19 centers around California and sold the company to the Washington Post, who funded our expansion to 165 centers nationwide.

The secret to our success in this business was hiring the right people, developing them, and giving them the vote of confidence and freedom to do their best work. We hired people who were young and mostly fresh out of college, but overqualified for their jobs based on their schooling, intelligence, ambition, communication skills, and creativity. We were able to recruit them not only due to favorable economic circumstances, but mainly because we provided them a sense of ownership in the creation of the company, a sense of meaning in their work, and a sense of belonging within a positive corporate culture. The people were completely the reason for our success. They ran with their responsibilities and opportunities and made the company great.

This early lesson has proved to be true again and again in my later ventures. I have made a few hiring decisions where I didn't apply the same high standards as I had at Score!, and they all came back to bite me. And when I held out on filling positions until I found stellar candidates who didn't necessarily have the required nuts and bolts on their resumes but possessed the general attributes I mentioned, the results always far exceeded everyone's expectations.

My colleagues from Yale have echoed this learning. I remember an entrepreneur on a panel joking about how everyone had ignored organizational development courses in school and spent all their time on topics such as corporate finance, venture capital, and strategy. Later, he and his friends realized the people issues were the make-or-break factors for their businesses. He said he wished he had paid more attention in class. Just about every business leader in the room nodded.

I have since also realized the importance of recognizing individual strengths and giving people the space and support to do what they individually do best. We followed this practice at Score! without realizing it, but it is now clear to me that there are nine distinct strength areas from 1) making improvements to 2) meeting needs to 3) achieving a successful image. I outline all nine strength categories in *The Career Within You.*

Leaders can make the mistake of continuing to hire the same kind of person, trying to replicate the same success over and over, but most organizations need a well-rounded team that possesses all nine strengths. To invest in your organization's greatest asset, become aware of your own biases based on your own strengths, recruit for strengths diversity on your team, and support your people to take ownership of their areas and do what they do best.

Pick Your Co-Founders Wisely.

Alexandra Cavoulacos
Founder, The Muse
Angel Investor and Avid Cyclist

IF THERE IS ONE THING I WISH I HAD KNOWN WHEN I started my first company, it's how important my choice of co-founders would be. I worried about the size of the market we were entering, whether our idea was as innovative as we thought, even things as trivial as what our logo should look like. But I didn't really challenge myself to think about the other people with whom I was starting a company. We had come up with the idea together, so it was logical that we would build the company together—that only seemed right.

When our company fell apart ten months later, it wasn't due to the size of the market or because the idea wasn't innovative enough. It was because I hadn't asked the tough questions early on to see if I was embarking on this entrepreneurial journey with the right people. Yes, we were passionate about the same space, but we didn't have the same long-term vision for the company or, more importantly, the same values.

163

Losing that first company was incredibly painful, but it taught me an important lesson. Agreeing to start a company with someone is like getting married; you shouldn't do it lightly. You're in it for the long haul, and you can't end that relationship quickly or painlessly.

When I started The Daily Muse (now known as The Muse), I applied that lesson. I now have two incredible co-founders who not only share my values and vision, but on whom I can rely through thick and thin. We have complementary skills, honest and frequent communication, and a phenomenal relationship. I know it is on these strong foundations that we'll build a successful company with a culture I am proud of.

So, as you embark on your own entrepreneurial journey, make sure to pick your partners wisely and to ask the tough questions up front. Because when things get tough, and when you hit those exciting highs, you'll be so glad you did.

Like Good Friends.

J.B. Schramm
Founder and CEO, College Summit

LOOK FOR PARTNERS WHO HAVE THE SAME CHARAC-teristics I've taught my children to look for in a good friend:

- ⇨ Someone who makes you stronger
- ⇨ Someone who is trustworthy
- ⇨ Someone who laughs

BE SHAMELESS BUT GENUINE ABOUT NETWORKING

Be Shameless—But Genuine—About Networking.

Jonathan Swanson
Co-Founder and President, Thumbtack.com

THERE ARE MANY IMPORTANT QUALITIES YOU NEED in order to excel in the startup scene—scrappiness, contagious enthusiasm, and willingness to undertake an enormous amount of not-always glorious work. But those characteristics are often innate and difficult to learn. Being shameless about networking is an easy practice to pick up, and the earlier you start, the more you will gain.

It's this simple: make a list of a few dozen people you want to meet, and send them an earnest and genuine email asking for their advice. Repeat—forever. Some people will ignore your email, but you will be surprised by how many very prominent people will respond and be willing to help. Be diligent about sending thank you emails, following up with updates, and reconnecting when the time is right. Be genuine, and offer to help them whenever you can. Some conversations will be dead ends, but many will be fruitful. Some won't show dividends immediately, but will prove valuable months or years later. Rand Fishkin calls this practice "manufacturing serendipity."

Before moving to San Francisco to start Thumbtack, I worked in the White House in D.C. When I moved to San Francisco, I didn't know anyone other than my co-founders. After a couple years of monomaniacal, singular, anti-social dedication to building my company, I decided it was time to venture out and meet more people.

For the last year, I've made a point of always inviting people over to lunch, meeting people for breakfasts, hosting dinner parties, and attending meetups. It requires a real investment of time and money. But it's enormously rewarding. I've not only made an incredible number of useful business contacts, I've also made some amazing friendships.

Wisdom Based on Experience.

Peter O. Crisp
Founder and former Managing Partner, Venrock Associates

SURROUND YOURSELF WITH PEOPLE WHO ARE smarter than you and have passion, drive, judgment—and integrity. Then give them scope to perform and succeed.

Finding Your Team.

Eugene A. Ludwig
Founder and CEO, Promontory Financial Group
Former U.S. Comptroller of the Currency under President Clinton
Vice Chairman and Senior Control Officer, Bankers Trust/Deutsche Bank,
Partner, Covington & Burling LLP

ENTREPRENEURSHIP REQUIRES MORE THAN A NOVEL idea or a better process, and it demands more than inspiration. It requires both successful execution and a team.

I did not spend most of my career running a business. I moved to Washington after my time at Yale and started a career in banking law. President Clinton, who had been a friend at Oxford and at Yale, asked me to help pull the nation out of a historic credit crunch and get the banking system back on its feet.

It is hard not to appreciate the magnitude of a task like that, and very quickly you begin to realize that your success or failure depends on factors outside of your control. You rely on policymakers elsewhere in government who must support your work; on the political winds, which must blow at your back; and most of all, on your colleagues who must help you turn the president's policies into reality.

When I had the opportunity to start a business ten years ago, I thought some aspects of it would be much simpler. Serving clients is no meager task, and as a lawyer, I was intimately familiar with how difficult it could be. But it was a task that appeared to have far fewer moving parts—you either do the work ably and fully, or you fail, entirely on your own terms. And of course, any job is much easier when your immediate supervisors aren't members of Congress.

Within a few months of founding Promontory, however, it became apparent that my colleagues were as important to our work as they were in government. Their substantive expertise was vital, of course, but their ideas were even more valuable. They challenged me when I was too sure I was right, and they bolstered me when I believed I had been wrong. They understood the challenges our clients faced in different ways. Together, we could offer a more complete picture of the road ahead than we ever could alone.

There is a temptation among entrepreneurs to believe everything should rest entirely on their own shoulders. I urge you to fight it. There is no decision more important than the people you choose to hire. Surround yourself with sharp minds and hard workers; open yourself to criticism, and seek it out when it isn't forthcoming. There is no surer way to make your work better or your days (and nights) at the office more rewarding.

Your Team Is Your Best Asset.

Brynne Herbert
Founder and CEO, MOVE Guides

WHEN I WAS STARTING MY BUSINESS, MOVE GUIDES, I wish someone had told me that the most difficult thing about building a business is hiring. I underestimated the challenge of finding the right people for MOVE Guides and the amount of time that it takes!

The Key to Hiring.

Kevin Ryan
Founder & Chairman, Gilt, MongoDB, Business Insider, Zola

A CEO'S MOST IMPORTANT JOB IS MANAGING TALENT, and a company's most valuable asset is its employees. Do not put too high a value on a résumé; a résumé helps establish basic qualifications, but not much else. If there is one piece of advice I can share, it is to improve your hiring process by using references.

Hiring is not an exact science. Even though I have hired about as many people as anyone out there, I still occasionally make mistakes. Reflecting back on these mistakes, I often determine that the root cause of the mistake is that I did not spending enough time doing reference checks.

Reference checking is the number one thing that business owners and hiring managers do not spend enough time doing. They're often willing to interview fifty candidates, which translates to approximately fifty hours of trying to find someone to fill the role. But how many people do you know who are willing to spend five hours doing follow-up reference checks?

Someone knows the person you are interviewing, and they know in incredible detail whether or not this person will do a good job and be a right fit for the team, the company, and the culture. You need to dig up that person and have a candid conversation.

If you have the choice between being able to interview more candidates or conducting reference checks, it's more important to do reference checks.

It's Still About the People.

Bob Casey
Founder and CEO, YouRenew

IN EARLY 2008, DURING MY SOPHOMORE YEAR AT Yale, I applied for a Yale Entrepreneurial Institute (YEI) Summer Fellowship as the founder of Ambrosia Brands. With Ambrosia, we wanted to bring healthy energy drinks to market to compete with sugary, unhealthy beverages. My co-founder and I spent most of our meager savings hiring a beverage chemist, developing a logo and branding material, and conducting market research.

Jim Boyle, the Director of YEI, thought we were crazy. We had no experience in the beverage industry—or any industry, for that matter—yet we were absolutely convinced that we could build a successful energy drink business. We had reams of market research, dozens of meetings with industry experts under our belt, and a product in development. Although Jim and his team could not fathom how we would succeed with Ambrosia, with utter persistence we were able to convince YEI to accept us as Fellows.

Two months after we were accepted into the program, and before the summer session even began, my team came to the same conclusion that Jim had reached months before: for a variety of reasons, Ambrosia was not going to work out. We trudged to Jim's office and shared our realizations. We had a new idea that involved recycling mobile phones, but we were not sure if YEI would allow us to remain as Fellows given our last-minute pivot.

Jim was surprised by our overnight about-face—we had shown absolute conviction in Ambrosia only weeks before. After asking a few pointed questions, however, he assured us that we were still welcome as summer fellows. Relieved, and more than a bit surprised, we hurried away without asking many more questions—and before Jim could change his mind.

Thankfully, our pivot into cell phone recycling seems to have paid off. Four years after we abandoned the beverage industry, our company, YouRenew, now processes tens of thousands of mobile phones each month for repair, recycling, and refurbishing on behalf of more than 300 enterprise clients, including dozens of Fortune 500 firms. We have reached this point only because we've assembled an incredible team of talented, adaptable, and driven people.

It took me awhile to understand, but Jim recognized that start-ups are really about people. He was betting on the founders rather than on any one idea we presented. At the end of the day, a company is just a collection of individuals organized to achieve a common goal—and more often than not, startup struggles are won or lost due to team dynamics, employee skillsets, and the ability to work together.

I had the immense fortune of starting my company and building our team while still an undergraduate, and YouRenew has, in many senses, been an extension of my Yale education. I've learned as much from my team and mentors as I ever did in a classroom.

I've come to realize the power of being a student and the value of surrounding yourself with experienced mentors and bright peers. This doesn't have to end at graduation. It is still all about the people. So seek out the best. Pick up the phone and reach out to someone you admire. Share your enthusiasm and passion, build an amazing team—and the amazing company will follow.

Two Seconds.

Mara Segal

VP, Product and Marketing, Samsung Accelerator
Founder and CEO, Utique Inc. (U*tique)

CONSUMERS TODAY ARE FLOODED; ATTENTION spans are shorter. What does this mean for reaching them? If we are lucky, we have two seconds with them—one to get their attention and one to tell them why we matter.

We compete in an increasingly crowded marketplace. New technologies come to market quickly, inexpensively, and with functional parity amongst a competitive set. The implication: entrepreneurs and companies need to rely on other attributes of differentiation to build recognition, evangelism, and stickiness with their consumers. What becomes important in consumer-facing markets is the ability to deepen understanding of your consumer and provide the higher order benefits they seek (going beyond what it can do to how it makes them feel and their connection to the values of your brand). Consumer insight, brand strategy, and design are great tools to deliver on this need.

I started my career as a brand strategist in "the Olympics of marketing"—categories like beverage and beauty. In these categories, there were iconic brands, a thick density of offerings, and multiple products with identical value propositions. We needed to rely on our ability to decode consumers, tapping into deeper motivations, integrating into their lifestyles, and providing carefully nuanced offerings to build relevance. Every touch point of the brand was important in building relevance and clarity of purpose—all communications, identity, packaging, experiential details of the product, tonality of customer service, and more.

When building U*tique (the company I founded in 2007), my brand strategy background and (architectural) design education at Yale became an advantage in value creation; complex things needed to be communicated visually, and with maximum impact to capture the consumer's attention and relay the message. Our product's design became a key mechanism for gaining recognition and driving revenues and partnerships. Despite our small size (one location), we broke through. People took pictures with our product and placed them in their social media feeds. Magazines from around the world contacted us to run features. We didn't need to spend our precious resources on marketing, as the product and our evangelist consumers did the trick. Most importantly, we stood out amongst peers and earned the consumers' business and respect.

After exploring various methods of driving innovation and developing new products, I have made more relevant products when I've understood the consumer (pain) first and not lost touch with them on the development journey (vs. technology pushes). I have also seen consistent ROI from investing in design (get noticed, see it spread).

Consumers today are flooded and have limited attention spans. We have two seconds with them—one to get their attention and one to tell them why we matter. With strong design and a deep understanding of what makes a product and brand relevant for them, you are more likely to cut through the clutter and build a lasting relationship.

Let Your Customers Teach You.

Anna Barber
Co-Founder and CEO, Scribble Press

WHEN YOU ARE FIRST DREAMING UP YOUR IDEA, YOU will think you know what your product or service should do, who will use it, how it will look, and how much it should cost. If you expect to raise money, you'll certainly have to present those initial details—including what the product, delivery method, and pricing structure will look like—to potential investors.

However, it's important to understand that the product you ultimately produce and offer will be totally different twelve months later from whatever you put in that initial presentation. Because as you develop your product or service, your customers will tell you what they want, how it should look, what they'll pay for it, and where they want it delivered. The earlier and the better you can listen to your customers, the better your results are going to be.

The best approach is to think of each stage in launching your business as an experiment. What is the hypothesis you are testing at each phase, and how quickly and cheaply can you get some readable results?

There are many benefits to the test-and-learn approach to building a business. Here are a few of them:

⇨ If your idea doesn't work, you'll know more quickly than if you spend a year designing the product and launching it, only to have it fail spectacularly. "Fail early and often" if you want to be a successful entrepreneur.

⇨ You will use your financial resources more sparingly with this approach, committing to incremental expenditures as you proceed.

⇨ You will make your customers your partners throughout development, not an obstacle to be overcome or an audience to convince once the product has been launched.

⇨ You will train yourself to be humble and to be a student of everything around you.

Success doesn't come from having better ideas or working harder than others. It comes from being a better listener to what the market—and your customers—are telling you—at every stage along the way.

BEING THE BEST.

ACCOMPLISH SOMETHING

every DAY

Accomplish Something Every Day.

Richard Thalheimer
Founder and former CEO, The Sharper Image
Founder, RichardSolo.com

MOST PEOPLE WANT A BALANCE BETWEEN PERSONAL life and work life. That makes sense, and we should all strive to get that balance. Having said that, if you want to be very successful in your chosen career, you want to ask yourself every morning, *"What can I accomplish today to help me move closer to reaching my goals?"*

If you don't do *anything* that particular day to move closer to your goals—however small an accomplishment it may be—then you have effectively wasted that day. You really did not accomplish anything that day, in terms of your entrepreneurial goals.

Most people have a lot of days where nothing really gets accomplished in terms of moving forward. So for many people, success in business will remain elusive.

If you have your own business or profession, accomplishing something may be as small as getting a new business account, making cold calls, improving your technology knowledge or systems, adding some resource or equipment ... you get the idea.

If you are working a job for another company, accomplishing something may be finishing a project, visiting with your boss (talk about how you can take on more responsibility), polishing your resume, applying for a class of some sort, or just doing a really good job with the clients you are meeting.

To help you in making sure you are on the right track, ask yourself in the morning, "*What might I do today to move my career forward?*"

At the end of the day, ask yourself, "*Did I accomplish something, whether big or small, that helped me move forward today?*"

It helps to remember that some days are *big* days, others are small accomplishments, but the important thing is to get something done *today!*

Life is a marathon, not a sprint. Doing something every day, with consistency, will add up to a great result down the road. It may take years, but the constant effort to accomplish something every day will add up to a very successful career.

Three Essentials to a Company's Success.

Lauren Monahan
Co-Founder, UPPAbaby

WHEN OUR CHILDREN WERE YOUNG, MY HUSBAND and I found that the juvenile gear on the market was either unappealing (with cartoons, colors, and materials that weren't especially sophisticated), or over-designed and priced well out of reach for the majority of parents. We saw a space and need in the market for strollers and car seats that were safe and comfortable for children, but that also appealed to parents through modern design and good value. As we continue to develop new products, we start by asking the same basic question: Is there a true need for what I want to sell?

Assuring that your product fits a gap between existing product offerings is critical. It could be a revolutionary item, a different type of relationship you are offering to your customer, or perhaps both. The differences between your product and those that currently exist may be subtle, but you must be able to carve out a distinct space in the marketplace or there will be no reason for a customer to choose you and your product over a company or brand that is already established.

My husband, Bob, has a strong engineering, finance, and operations background. My experience falls more in the sales, marketing, and legal realms. We have different yet very complementary skillsets, and we have assembled a team of people who are highly talented in areas we feel are critical to our company. It's imperative to choose carefully when you build your team. Invest most in the key areas that drive your business. Our vice president of design has a strong and clear industrial design vision. He incorporates a clean, modern aesthetic that he consistently communicates through all of our products and materials. Our director of customer service is easygoing and warm. She has a knack for calming people down, then offering them a fair and generous resolution to their concerns. She expects the same from her employees in our customer service department, the largest area of our company. Our office manager is extremely approachable and a very hard worker. People feel comfortable talking to her, enabling her to provide constant feedback regarding our employee morale and needs. She models an easygoing attitude and strong work ethic. These are just a few examples of our team, their talents, and the personalities that make our company successful.

Lastly, it's essential to believe in whatever you are selling, but you cannot lose sight of how you treat your customers. Your product may be outstanding, but it's only part of the equation. Your customers must feel respected and supported. If not, they will settle for a lesser product from a company they prefer. We talk to end users directly each day from our corporate office, and our company is known for being easy to reach and highly responsive. When people buy baby products, they rely heavily on advice from their friends. Our very happy customers highly recommend our products and our company. How we treat our customers has gained us their loyalty and built our brand.

A Venture Culture.

Robert S. Adelson
Managing Partner, Osage Partners

OUR FIRM, OSAGE PARTNERS, MANAGES TWO VEN-
ture funds. The first, Osage Venture Partners, provides early-stage
financing to enterprise software companies. The second, Osage University Partners, invests in university spinoffs in all technologies and
at all stages of development in partnership with forty-six of the leading national research universities.

We have tried to develop a venture culture that emphasizes a
number of elements we think are crucial to business success and personal fulfillment at work.

THESE INCLUDE:

⇨ Investing (and deciding where to work): Value flows from
   choosing the right sector, team, and product, in that order.
⇨ Sector: Embrace risk. Be contrarian, and look for disruptive, not incremental, improvements.
⇨ Team: At our firm, and at our portfolio companies, it is all
   about the talent. "A" leaders hire A+ talent; "B" leaders hire

C talent. Judge people by the team they build. If you are the smartest person in the room, and remain so for more than a few months, start to worry.

⇨ Product: The tried-and-true way to judge a product's value is by the customer's second purchase. Many products are over-engineered, some are too incremental to displace legacy products, and others solve too narrow a problem. The best solutions offer value through simplicity and target the highest priority needs of buyers.

IN TERMS OF OUR VENTURE CULTURE:

⇨ Preparation. Before meeting with an entrepreneur, our team members always read everything that we have received about the proposed business. Before interviewing a candidate for our firm or for one of our portfolio companies, we always review the person's resume and related background information. Although this sounds like a small issue, we think preparation not only improves our performance, it is also a mark of respect for the people with whom we meet.

THIS LEADS TO ANOTHER CULTURAL TOUCH POINT:

⇨ Respect. We do not make people who come to our office wait for us—we start our meetings on time. We give a full hearing for all presentations, even if we know early on that the investment is not a fit for us. And we do our best to give our best advice/most honest reaction at the end of the meeting. Like other venture firms, we invest in no more than one-half percent of the opportunities we see. Therefore, we believe respecting the many entrepreneurs who we will not fund means giving them our undivided attention and the benefit of our experience.

⇨ Modesty. In the venture business, wealth is created by entrepreneurs who have the insight and the talent to take a nascent idea and build it into a successful company. Venture capitalists can and do help some of those companies in many ways, but at our firm, we try to remember that the role we play in value creation is secondary to that of the initial risk-taker.

⇨ Honesty. Finally, be brutally honest with yourself about your strengths and weaknesses, and particularly about the latter. The sooner you recognize your personal deficits, the sooner you can structure your work life to ensure the best possible outcome.

Intuition vs. Emotion.

Ben Jacobs
Co-Founder and CEO, Whistle

IN THESE EARLY STAGES OF OUR COMPANY, THE MOST concise and interesting piece of advice I received from one of our mentors was around what he called "Intuition vs. Emotion."

At any small and growing company, you have to make decisions quickly and with incomplete information. Small business owners and technology entrepreneurs often talk about "gut" or "hunch" that guided them down a certain path during pivotal points for the organization. As a younger CEO, this particularly feels like the case.

But it's important to distinguish that feeling from fact-based hypotheses. If you make decisions based purely on emotion—whether negative ones like fear, anger, disappointment, or positive ones like excitement, joy, even love—your decisions will be entirely gut, and you'll often overreact or over-adjust in a moment of crisis.

The best founders have an incredible, perhaps natural, ability to act on intuition rather than emotion. They evaluate critical situations and make key decisions in real-time, but do so without letting pure emotion cloud their process. This ability is something I'm still trying to harness myself—as I am driven in our business by passion.

That's my two cents.

I'd also add that "entrepreneurs" have many forms, and I have utmost respect for anyone trying to build something new, whether on their own or in a larger organization, in tech or otherwise. And hopefully they have as much fun with, and learn as much from, their team as I do. I feel extremely fortunate to work with the smartest, kindest, and most humble people I know.

Constant Striving.

Rohini B. Shah
Founder, Blu Salt

ENTREPRENEURSHIP IN MODERN LEXICON IS EM-blematic of the brilliant trailblazer, the unrelenting perfectionist, and the natural born leader. I say this is rubbish. Yes, there are the Steve Jobs and the Mark Zuckerbergs of the world—but entrepreneurship is just as embodied in the first generation immigrant dry cleaner or food cart owner. There is no less vision, calculated risk bearing, fiscal prudence, and sheer hard work in establishing a successful, productive business at this scale than there is in any other. Regardless of the scale of success, each of these businesses has some very important traits in common.

The vision of the entrepreneurial multi-billionaire is an enticing, but deeply flawed one—mainly because it masks the true path of entrepreneurial success. Inherently, the higher probability of success in entrepreneurship stems from the ability to build a product or service for a perceived market need and then constantly work on improving it to better meet the needs of your customers. It is an almost Zen-like approach to continuous self-improvement since it requires a great deal of diligence and humility to adhere to—the success follows automatically. Focusing on the results, as in most endeavors in life, belittles the incremental progress that is necessary and makes the path to success seem dauntingly long.

Your interest in entrepreneurship should be lauded, for it takes a certain individual of self-confidence and industry to choose the path less traveled. However, the importance of marrying that self-confidence with humility to recognize that you, in the end, are serving a customer should not be underestimated.

You Must Love Lamarcus Thompson.

Winston Bao Lord
Co-Founder and CMO, Venga

WHAT DO YOU THINK IT TAKES TO BE A SUCCESSFUL entrepreneur? Here's my list:

#1 POSSESS AN INNATE DRIVE.

You either have it or you don't. My whole team does.

#2 PICK YOUR CO-FOUNDER CAREFULLY AND COMPLEMENTARY.

Not all startups need a co-founder. I certainly did. My co-founder, Sam, and I worked for four years together at Portfolio Logic. We have complementary skills—he's the business/business model guy (I went to school pretty much before computers). He WASN'T a close friend outside of the work environment, but I knew he was someone I could trust. I knew he would be in the trenches with me (several times we struggled to meet payroll, and he had opportunities to get a full-time job).

#3 EVOLVE OFTEN AND FAIL FAST.

Two months after launching our first generation product, we knew it wasn't working and wouldn't last. We could have held on or moved on and adapted. We chose the latter.

#4 HANDLE UNCERTAINTY WITH APLOMB.

You must be a BIG fan of LaMarcus Thompson (a developer of roller coasters in the late 1800s), because there are so many highs and lows. I've never experienced lower lows, and I'm sure there are many more to come.

#5 LISTEN AND LEARN

(AKA build something the industry "wants,"
not what you think the industry "needs").

We've surrounded ourselves with people smarter than us.

#6 HAVE FUN AND WORK WITH PEOPLE WHO SHARE YOUR CULTURE.

Life is too short not to do something you're passionate about. As important, make sure you're doing it with people you'd go to the ends of the world for. We were charmed by an investor who was "perfect on paper." He'd recently sold his restaurant tech company for $100 million, had a great sales track record, offered to put money in when we were out of money, but did not fit our values and culture. As hard as it was, we turned him down. We're better and stronger for it.

Execution Is Everything.

Scott C. Johnston
Co-Founder, Wayin LLC

IF YOU'VE SEEN *THE SOCIAL NETWORK*, YOU KNOW about the Winklevoss twins, who famously claimed they were the ones who originally had the idea for Facebook. Frankly, they probably did, but so what? Does anyone think they could have turned their idea into the $30 billion company that Facebook is today? In the end, they were well compensated, but not anywhere near Mark Zuckerberg. And that seems about right.

What I'm getting at is that great ideas are maybe the smallest component of entrepreneurial success. Seems wrong, doesn't it? After all, the idea is what gets you fired up. But, really, great ideas are a dime a dozen. I probably have ten in my head right now, but, again, so what?

Execution is so much more important. Raising capital, hiring (and keeping) the right people, setting up operations, dealing with regulatory compliance, making sales, customer relations. It is highly complex, and a misstep in any area can sink the ship. This is why many entrepreneurs don't end up running the companies they start, because the creative skillset doesn't always overlap with the operational skillset. It's also why many great companies weren't actually the first to come up with the ideas that now seem wholly theirs. These companies took existing ideas and out-executed. Apple did not invent the digital music player or the smartphone. Google did not invent search. It's a long list.

Think of an idea, get excited, but then think long and hard about all the not-so-fun stuff. Execution separates the winners from the losers.

Gifting.

Dave Lieberman
Chef, TV Host, and Bestselling Cookbook Author

GIVE GIFTS FREELY AND OFTEN. THE VALUE AND IM-
portance of showing appreciation through small, thoughtful gifts is a
habit that took me too long to acquire.

Sending thoughtful and timely tokens of appreciation is something that all of the best entrepreneurs I have worked with have in
common. So, when even the slightest frisson of gratitude comes
upon you, take a moment to send a little something to the person
who has been good to you.

It will come back in spades.

Living

─ THE ─

80/20

RULE

Living the 80/20 Rule.

Mike Del Ponte
Founder and CEO, Soma

EIGHTY PERCENT OF RESULTS COME FROM 20% OF IN-puts. Whether that's 80% of revenue coming from 20% of your clients or 80% of your happiness coming from 20% of your relationships, this is a powerful truth that should be lived, not merely acknowledged.

I recently heard a quote that is so true, both in our personal and professional lives: "Successful people procrastinate with small things. Unsuccessful people procrastinate with big things." What are the big things in your life and business that you've been putting off? What are the small things you're wasting your time doing? What can you eliminate from your life or delegate to others?

At Soma, we are constantly reflecting on the 80/20 Rule. We identify the projects that are bearing the most fruit. We make lists of things to delegate and create systems to automate the small, but required tasks. We do less, but achieve more.

The Perfection of Imperfection.

Mie-Yun Lee
Managing Director, Reed Business Information
Founder, BuyerZone

EVERYONE WARNED ME THAT STARTING A BUSINESS would be really hard and would take a lot of work. They were absolutely right. Twenty years later, I see that my journey could have been much easier if someone had told me this: strive for imperfection.

By striving for imperfection, you can get your offering out to the market faster. Don't wait for that next thing you need to do before you can release it. Let the market tell you what needs to be worked on instead of you spending too much time addressing flaws that don't exist. Once it's good enough, get going and start improving from there.

Also, starting a business demands more hours than anyone has time to give. As a result, you won't be able to do everything you should do and certainly not all the things you could do. You will get farther faster by spending the right level of effort against each item on your "to do" list. While some activities will require close to perfection, seek imperfection where it matters less, so you can have more time and energy to cover more items faster.

Finally, starting a business means you will make lots of mistakes—big ones, small ones, funny ones, and downright embarrassing ones. And, as the boss, you will know about ALL of them. There is no hiding. By striving for imperfection, you can take this in stride. Rather than spending too much energy beating up yourself or others, or slowing things down trying to do everything perfectly, you can just roll with it, address the situation, and move on.

To be clear, doing things poorly is never acceptable. But as a perfectionist, I see that even if my journey starting, growing, and selling BuyerZone had not been any different, simply changing my attitude would have made it more satisfying and enjoyable. Embrace the perfection of imperfection.

What All Entrepreneurs Share.

Jessica Jewell Ogilvie
Co-Founder, AdBuyer.com

I'M OFTEN ASKED WHAT TYPE OF PERSON MAKES A successful entrepreneur. If you had asked me ten years ago, I wouldn't have pegged myself as "the type." But since founding my first company in 2007 and being an early employee at two more startups, I've learned that early-stage entrepreneurs come in all forms and share some key characteristics.

Entrepreneurs are resilient. You are going to be rejected. You are going to fail. No one raises money from every investor. No first version of a product is going to be a breakout hit. The key is to learn from these experiences and to not take them personally.

Entrepreneurs are gritty. Nothing is beneath you as a founder. You are going to have to do things that aren't glamorous. Whether it is assembling office furniture or being the person behind the curtain of a concierge MVP, you need to be willing to roll up your sleeves as much or more than anyone else on your team.

Entrepreneurs adapt. It's a rarity for a business to follow its original business plan. The best entrepreneurs listen to the market, talk to users, and look deeply at their metrics. They learn what's working and what's not, and then they adapt. They don't dig their heels into their original idea.

Entrepreneurs execute and know the power of having executors on their team. The bottom line is you need to get stuff done and surround yourself with people who get stuff done.

Lastly, successful early-stage entrepreneurs benefit from a co-founder they trust. Are your skills complementary? Are your incentives aligned? Do you have a shared vision? The decision of who to partner with is one of the most critical a founder will face.

The Value We Each Bring.

Louise Langheier
CEO, Co-Founder of Peer Health Exchange

I WAS TWENTY-TWO YEARS OLD AND HAD JUST GRAD-uated from Yale when I co-founded Peer Health Exchange in 2003. My co-founder and I had a lot of big ideas, an enormous amount of passion, and just a few gaps in experience. I learned quickly that you can get a lot of help when you make it clear what you do and don't know, and that filling in your own gaps with the experience of incredible people is fundamental to future success.

The first investors in Peer Health Exchange's work (who also happened to be Yale alumni) were the best possible example of that talent—committing resources, their brains, their time, their friends, and their high expectations. They made me believe that this kind of help should be the standard, modeling how supporters can invest themselves alongside resources, giving me the confidence to go out and seek it for many years to come.

I have taken that lesson with me as Peer Health Exchange has grown. I continue to see the importance of building the best team you can and empowering that team to do its best possible work. A core value at Peer Health Exchange is "agency," through which we recognize the value each of us brings to our work. By empowering our team to lead, I've been challenged, humbled, and inspired to continue pushing our work to new heights. As we set our sights on more ambitious goals, I look to the people around me as the vehicle that will get us there.

So Many Stones.

Jordan Goldberg
Co-Founder and CEO, stickK

THE MOST IMPORTANT LESSON I CAN RELAY TO THE next generation of entrepreneurs is this: most of the trite words of wisdom you hear from more experienced entrepreneurs are actually true. But so few people pause to reflect upon their meaning. "Be passionate." "Focus." "Execution is everything."

One of my favorites is a phrase we've all heard many times: "Do one thing, and do it really well." I never stopped to think about what that really meant. It sounds simple, but it is not.

As an entrepreneur, it is tempting to bite off more than you can chew. Don't. You can inch along at several things at once, or move miles at a time at one thing. It is easy to entertain every invitation for a cup of coffee or pint of beer. It is easy to be swayed in new directions. What separates great entrepreneurs from the pack is how they use their time and energy. I'm still trying to figure it out.

You've heard the phrase, "Leave no stone unturned." That is true for many aspects of life. Not entrepreneurship. Pick the right stones. Leave the rest where they are.

THE PATH IS NOT ALWAYS STRAIGHT.

Why Work Is
a Four-Letter Word.
(How I Found Work I Love and Why
It Took Me So Long to Figure It Out)

Chris DeVore
General Partner, Founders Co-op
Managing Director of Techstars Seattle

MY JOB IS RIDICULOUSLY FUN. ALL DAY, EVERY DAY, I meet with incredibly smart and passionate people who are working to invent a piece of the future. They all have a vision for how the world can be different and better, and my job is to find some way to help them. It wasn't always this way.

I had no idea what I wanted to do when I got out of college. All my life I had thought of education and work as separate domains—learning was a commercial-free zone dedicated to ideas and discovery; work was something you had to do to make money. If you were really lucky, your work might have broader significance—my dad was a First Amendment lawyer and was passionate about the principle of free speech—but that kind of work was rare and not to be expected.

Because I didn't see the relationship between my education and my future working life, I studied subjects I was naturally drawn to— language and culture, history and human behavior—not ones that would help me get a job. And when I graduated from college, I didn't have a clue what to do next.

Somehow, I talked my way into an entry-level job at a small management consulting firm. I didn't know the first thing about business, and I spent two years in a state of constant confusion about what I was doing and why it mattered. One of our clients—a huge public company—recruited me to join them full-time, and I spent two more years learning how even admired brands do crummy things to make a buck, and how much of the "work" at big companies is internal squabbling over power and money with no real concern for the company or its customers. I still had no idea what I wanted my work to look like, but I was getting clearer about what I didn't want, and that was a start.

By another random turn of events, I found a job at a startup and encountered a radically new idea: entrepreneurial companies weren't big stable things you worked for or consulted to; they were messy, chaotic things you made, and the process of making them was exciting—and fun. I worked for that company for almost two years ... until we were acquired by the same big company I had worked for previously. So I started looking for something new.

I now understood that I was happier working at smaller companies and had a growing conviction that I should actually care about what business I was in. By coincidence, I heard about a job opening at a company I had always admired and whose products I used and liked. I wasn't really qualified for the role, but I was passionate about it. Somehow, I talked them into hiring me. It was the hardest job I've ever had, and the one in which I learned the most about business and leadership. It also gave me a chance to do something I had never done before, and set me on the path I've been following ever since. I brought with me to that business a passion for this new thing called the Internet, and in my second year at the company, 1995, I convinced them they should be selling their goods online and invented a new job for myself running that business.

I left for business school two years later, and have had many work-related adventures since then, but my early career "mistakes" were my most important learning experiences. Instead of thinking of work as a stable, pre-existing system to which I had to adapt myself, I came to understand it as a dynamic, creative exercise in which I had as much right of authorship as anyone else. Not only did this change in attitude transform my conception of work, it also altered the role that work came to play in my life. If I was the author of my own work, it was no longer something that sat outside my "real" life—it now sat at the center, and my satisfaction and sense of meaning in work was entirely up to me.

My only regret is that it took me so long to figure out that my dream job isn't out there waiting for me to find it; it's something I get to make. My one piece of advice to younger people who are about to enter the working world: don't wait to start making yours.

Moving the Needle.

Kevin J. Delaney
Editor in Chief, Co-Founder and Co-President, Quartz

I EMBARKED UPON MY FIRST STARTUP RELATIVELY late in my career. At age thirty-nine, I left my employer of sixteen years to start Quartz, a global business-news website owned by Atlantic Media.

Management research suggests that the odds were stacked against me, as the most successful entrepreneurs start much younger. Steve Jobs, Mark Zuckerberg, Sergey Brin, and Larry Page are all clear examples of that. Research also suggests that entrepreneurs often have a track record of starting things while still kids. My wife, Lisbeth Shepherd, a serial social entrepreneur, for example, had founded several small environmental conservation clubs even before she got to college.

I, on the other hand, followed a professional trajectory that I suspect is not far from the hierarchy found in medieval trade guilds. I was an intern at *The Wall Street Journal* for two summers during college. Over the course of about twelve years, I worked my way from "staff reporter" to "senior special writer" to "deputy managing editor" to "managing editor," slowly gaining skills and responsibility.

That time working alongside exceptionally talented colleagues has served me well as an entrepreneur. I learned the trade at the highest level and gained experience alongside people I respect, wrestling skillfully with a wide spectrum of management, legal, and ethical challenges. The blue-chip brand made it easy for me to establish, over the years, a network of people it would have been hard to get access to otherwise.

But there are less traditional elements of my experience in a big organization without which I wouldn't have been prepared for the role of entrepreneur. The key one is that I had gravitated to areas of my industry and company that required more scrappiness and provided more opportunities for original creation. I worked on a startup TV station part-owned by *The Wall Street Journal*, on the journal's personal finance magazine not long after its creation, on its European reporting team at a time of ambitious expansion, and for the journal's Internet unit before the center of gravity had shifted away from the newspaper.

These experiences were all critical to my ability to roll up my sleeves and confidently enter an empty office to get to work figuring out what Quartz would be. They taught me to focus on what truly moves the needle for a business—something that's easy to forget about within a big organization. My time working on teams charged with innovating within the larger company was also essential to my credibility leading an Internet startup.

One takeaway from my own atypical entrepreneurial experience is that there is perhaps underappreciated value in first working within an established organization. But you have to commit yourself to being an entrepreneur within any group, however large and traditional it may be, and learn to focus on what moves the needle of change. Without doing that, it will be hard to know when a good startup opportunity presents itself. And it will be hard to convince others—and yourself—that you're truly up for it.

Learning Through Experience.

Lise Laurin
Founder, EarthShift, LLC

LIKE MANY ENTREPRENEURS, I DIDN'T START OFF AS
an entrepreneur out of college. Well, perhaps I did—I started a successful cleaning service when I was fifteen years old and no one would
hire me. The clients I gathered that year kept me employed for three
years, after which the chain of references kept me with employment
until I graduated. And while the knowledge and job satisfaction that
I gained during that time was valuable, it in no way prepared me for
running what I would find as a satisfying business.

I was lucky in my career path that my managers pushed me
into various business roles. I started off as a process engineer on the
production line at Intel, then moved into development and R&D.
Shortly after moving to a startup company, I was thrown into a marketing management role. I had little experience as a manager and
none in marketing. The small company was filled with great examples of what to do to motivate employees and customers as well as
what not to do.

As I moved through my career, I was able to add skills to support a startup company, including how to write a business plan, create a website, do direct mail and direct e-mail campaigns, set up (and shut down) a company, create meaningful procedures, hire and manage a sales team, and more. So after eighteen years, when I found myself unemployed on a Thursday, I hung out my shingle the following Monday as a high tech marketing services company. My company relied on my eighteen years' experience in the high tech industry, along with skills in conducting market research, writing press releases and trade journal articles, and even desktop publishing. Still, I learned some things the hard way.

Now, two companies later, I have a company that supports industry in its endeavor to become more sustainable. Fifteen years ago when I started, I relied on many of the same skills that I used to start my first two companies. As time has passed, I realize that my time in manufacturing and my time learning what drives companies to make decisions have been even more valuable. When we make a hire right out of university, we find this understanding is missing—and it's nearly impossible to teach.

I could imagine having started a company right out of school, but it would have been one working with consumers on something not very technical. I think I would have gotten bored very quickly. By working in industry for a period of time, I gained valuable skills that I can now happily apply on a daily basis to doing what I love.

Making Decisions.

Rick Field
CEO, Rick's Picks

WHEN I GRADUATED FROM YALE WITH AN ENGLISH degree in 1985 ("practically fluent," as I told friends), I headed for New York City to enter the world of film and television with every intention of becoming the next great Sundance Film Festival success story, or at least the next great Nike commercial director. While I had my moments, particularly when working for VH1 as a promo director and later as a producer for Bill Moyers, I never really felt like I'd found my place.

Childhood experiences making pickles with my family during Vermont summers had left a deep impression and many fond memories, and as I toiled in the world of media and infotainment, I rekindled my interest in pickling. Over the course of seven years, the interest became a major hobby and later a serious obsession. Then, in the span of a few months, I turned forty, lost my job at Moyers, broke up with my girlfriend ... and won a pickle contest: Best in Show at the 2001 Rosendale International Pickle Contest. To my surprise, the following year I took home the Big Blue Ribbon again. My shrink saw this as a sign.

And so, less than a year later, under the banner of Rick's Picks, I began to hawk my products at Union Square Greenmarket. It was entrepreneurship in its purest form, not unlike, as I noted in glum moments, producing a low-budget independent film that never goes out of production.

There is always a crisis at hand or on the horizon, always a tough decision that needs to be made. It is *always something*. And it is up to you the entrepreneur, and you alone, to make decisions about how to tackle that something, whatever it might be. I observed that many of the dilemmas I had to face in TV resurfaced in the world of pickles, but in different forms. Over time, I developed some rules around these dilemmas and the decisions that get made as a result. The rules have served me very well and have a wide range of applications across many industries. The rules themselves are not complex to grasp, but the execution of the rules is where things can get tricky.

Rule number 1: *It always comes down to a decision between art and money.* You can have a beautiful product with the best ingredients and the most labor-intensive manufacturing practices, or you can have a simpler, cheaper product that is easier to make. TV executives always wanted to have their cake and eat it too: in their world it is called "champagne on a beer budget." The choice-making is even more articulated with a food product, but the parallels are easy to see. And this is not to say that one choice or the other is always going to be correct. It is a question of making the right choice for the business in each instance.

Example: organic produce runs 30-40% more, at least in ingredient costs, than produce that is not certified organic. I was committed to launching a brand with a spectrum of products (I launched with nine items, which was too many, but more about that in a second), and so I made that my focus instead of locally-sourced produce and all-natural products. In this case, it wasn't a case of choosing between two diametrically opposed choices, but the best option falling somewhere in the middle. As it often does.

Rule number 2: *Pay close attention to the power of threes.* Three is a very, very important number: one is an idea, two is a concept, but three is a campaign. In my promo days, most media campaigns we pitched had three iterations. Then consider products on a grocery shelf: one is an orphan, two is neither here nor there, but three products signal *a brand.* I could have started Rick's Picks with one-third of the products of the nine I did and still made an impact.

And back to the theme of decision-making. Any time you have three compelling arguments in alignment on a topic, you have a clear decision. Example: job candidate X is charming, will work for almost nothing, and knows a lot about pickles. Hire her!

Rule number 3: *The 85-15 rule.* This one is weighted to be more convincing than the standard 80-20 breakdown. The idea is that decision-making in the entrepreneurial realm can be paralyzing, and one needs to overcome one's own natural potential for paralysis. So the way to go is to build a solid body of evidence around a given decision, hopefully with three compelling reasons, and make sure you build this body of evidence in a fixed and finite period of time. Then make a decision you can live with long-term. The expectation is that 85% of your decisions are good ones, and the other 15% are good learning experiences that don't put you out of business.

These three rules are ones I've always followed, and thanks to the support of a lot of hard-working colleagues, devoted family, and supportive investors, Rick's Picks has had double-digit growth every year. We stared with confidence into an extremely bright horizon as we approached March 30, 2014, the tenth anniversary of the date that Rick's Picks, LLC was formed in the State of Delaware.

Maybe I'll make a movie about the whole experience someday if someone gives me three compelling reasons.

Follow the Old Soldier.

Alex Selkirk
Founder, Parlor
Founder, Common Data Project

I REMEMBER PEOPLE AT SCHOOL THINKING I KNEW what I was doing when I didn't. I realized that all of the jobs I was interviewing for were going to be lame and felt certain the only thing that would feel challenging enough was to start a company. It was clear my parents thought I should get a job, though, so at the time I felt I didn't have a choice. I needed to get a job.

I decided that the job I wanted wasn't sexy. It was at Microsoft. My best friend felt the need to remind me of the obvious, "They're the man, man." A friend of my parents told me to go talk to people in San Francisco. I talked my girlfriend into moving West with me— even though she had every reason to stay East … and no reason whatsoever to go West.

I interviewed with people who were afraid to take a chance on me. Then, I interviewed with people who were intimidated by me. Ultimately, I decided—against my better judgment—to go talk to a cocky startup in Mountain View. They were doing something I had already spent a lot of time thinking about.

I spent the day telling them what they were doing wrong. Then I learned a lot about why they had made the choices they did. As the day progressed, I met a lot of people I respected. Towards the end of the day I realized that they were going to offer me a job. Driving in traffic back to San Francisco, I concluded that I was unlikely to learn more anywhere else.

They set me up at a desk made out of a door from Home Depot, and I immediately felt at home. With my first paycheck, I bought a cell phone and made a down payment on a car. After I started working there, I had the highly original idea to secretly work on my own projects on the side. What those projects were wasn't important to me—my "strategy" was to pick something and work harder at it than anyone else.

True to form, the cocky startup was irreverent and fast. The world didn't yet know that we were going to change *everything*. Someone told me not to say I was looking for interesting tasks but rather that I wanted to focus on hard problems. I stopped working on my side projects because I started learning more in my "day job."

One day, a customer called me to find out how to pay us, and I realized I didn't know the answer. When I looked into it, I learned that it was not possible for customers to pay us. We ran a marathon, and then the gauntlet. When two-thirds of the company was laid off, I understood that we had hired irresponsibly. For the first time, I discovered that people were actually angry because they were not going to become rich. I was spared, but before I could revel in it, someone felt the need to tell me that there was a difference between being smart and being useful.

Later, I realized the product detour we had taken from the original vision was permanent. Listening to Neil Young, I thought, "twenty-four and there's so much more." I decided to leave when they were no longer willing to do anything that would take longer than a week to build.

It took me a year-and-a-half of triangulation to get the job I wanted at Microsoft. I wanted to experience the joy of being on-board an unstoppable locomotive … or a battleship … or the Death Star … and I did. They set me up at a real desk, in a real office, albeit windowless, and with an office mate. It was refreshing to be surrounded by a humble pride in accountability and competence. People took on hard problems in a happy, methodical way.

I received hundreds of emails every day that I had to deal with and began to grasp the black art of triage. I practiced persuasion and watched the stock price, hoping that our hard work would inch it upwards. Lost, driving with work friends, someone older and wiser pointed the way and said to me, "Follow the old soldier." I have been thinking about that statement ever since.

My girlfriend reminded me that it had been seven years since she agreed to spend two years on the West Coast. I reassured myself that I had already learned eighty percent of what I had come to learn. I remember realizing that, eight years after graduation, I was finally going to start a company. I decided that the company had to be interesting enough to attract the people I wanted to work with, which would make it doubly hard for the idea to succeed.

I moved back to New York, leaving all my West Coast connections behind, with my girlfriend-now-wife, because she needed to go back. I began working at a desk in my bedroom, sitting in an old barber's chair my wife bought for me at the thrift store. I deposited payments by walking to the bank and paid invoices with handwritten checks. I hired my first employee and got my first real taste of what it means to be responsible for someone else's livelihood.

At one point, I had the sudden awareness that my company's

reputation was on the line, and I was completely dependent on people whose reputations were not on the line. I began to think about how to productize our work and how to stabilize revenue. I met with dozens and dozens of people about where I should take the company, all of whom tried to tell me my ideas were naïve if not downright delusional. To stay sane, I ignored the things they said.

I worked harder to find people with the right knowledge and experience to be able to hear what I was saying, then harder still to find those who were able to judge it. I learned to tell the difference between feedback from people who simply lacked imagination and feedback from those who actually knew better than me.

I struggled to navigate the waters between self-delusion and fighting for something I believed in, discovering along the way that being the responsible one can be very unsatisfying. I spent political capital to force a business partner to do the right thing and learned how hard it is to keep the faith in something you still can't explain to anyone else. Then I understood—that's what makes someone a founder.

I began to hope that being scared sh*tless all the time wouldn't be the new status quo. Five years after leaving my last job to start a company, I saw the first glimmer of "getting somewhere," following the old soldier.

Kissing the Stanley Cup.

Bing Gordon
Partner, Kleiner Perkins
Former CCO, Electronic Arts

ONE OF MY PLEASURES IS WATCHING AND HELPING younger people develop from high potentials into young leaders. Former NHL hockey player and Wayne Gretzky roommate, Geoff Courtnall, once told me that the formula for winning the Stanley Cup was an equal measure of veterans who deliver and emerging rookies who overachieve. I believe that most healthy organizations, like hockey teams, need the excitement and energy of youth.

In ice hockey, as in life, hall of fame careers usually start fast. Wayne Gretzky was the NHL MVP at age nineteen, and Bill Gates, the Gretzky of software, founded Microsoft at age twenty. If you are a "high draft choice" in life, you have some responsibility to focus your gifts. It isn't just athletes who fail to live up to their early potential. I have always had regrets that I didn't start working in business until I was twenty-eight. I always felt just a little behind the power curve.

After decades of hiring and promoting high school and college grads, I have seen that those who get the most opportunities also start fast. They overachieve in their first weeks. They ask the best questions, and always seem to have good ideas bubbling out of them. And, as one successful Hollywood producer once told an entry-level agent, "Work as hard as you can, and then work harder."

On reflection, there are a few things I did well in my twenties. I lived the "liberal arts life," the most priceless education, wandering through several careers and geographies. But for a few twists of fate, I could just as easily have been a commercial fisherman in Australia as a videogame vice-president of marketing.

So I say, "Try stuff." Figure out what you like doing every day, and then always achieve within the possibilities of the stuff you love to do. Live up to Yale's high bar, because "playing in the pros" is even more demanding than college. Be optimistic and energetic every day. It's surprising how far this will take you. In the networked world, opportunities come to those who empower others.

But there are also a few things I wish I had done differently. The number one piece of advice I would share is to recruit a mentor. Find someone you admire who is at least one generation older and has no direct authority over you. Lack of context and perspective can cost you months and years, with a bad career choice, an unwise relocation, short-term negotiating posture, and, generally speaking, sophomoric thinking. Jeff Brenzel, Dean of Admissions at Yale, has the best advice on how to recruit a mentor: "All professors desire acolytes; so carry the favorite book of theirs under your arm and go introduce yourself with a question about their book."

Find heroes and study them closely. My business hero was the adman David Ogilvy because he was a writer and researcher, as well as business founder, and he wrote books to pass along his knowledge. For many new Internet entrepreneurs, Jeff Bezos of Amazon is a great choice. Read all the shareholder letters from Amazon's annual reports. Reid Hoffman wrote a cool book, *The Startup of You*. John

Madden wrote books about football, a syllabus about coaching, and inspired a twenty-five-year videogame franchise. An achiever who explains can be your pole star.

Gain knowledge in two areas, not one. You will find that many innovations arise at the intersection of disciplines—like videogames, genetics, electronic books, iPhones, and hip-hop. Be a lifelong learner, and never shut out feedback. And, while you're at it, become conversant in the computer science of data structures, statistics, and user interface. They are manipulatives of your future.

Finally, write down your ideas and plans, then take them out and reflect on them several times yearly. Memory lies, and misremembering is a weak foundation for education. Intellectual laziness puts your life at risk.

And, one last thing … if you are lucky, pay your luck forward to the next generation, and the next. Giving is the gift that keeps on giving.

PERSEVERANCE.

There Is A Way!

Mark T. Volchek
Founder and CEO, Higher One

EVERY ENTREPRENEUR WILL RUN INTO OBSTACLES when starting a new venture. Success is often determined by how these obstacles are navigated and overcome. Being creative and thinking outside the box is key. At Higher One, we have always believed "there is a Way." When we ran into dead ends that had no out, we found a way to get through anyway.

If a wall is blocking the way, I would consider going over or through the wall, rather than backtracking and starting over. Entrepreneurs usually break new ground to make their venture a success, so knowing how others have done things is good, but finding your own way is more important. Never give up! A venture only fails when the entrepreneurs give up!

On Failure.

Matthew O. Brimer
Co-Founder, General Assembly

WHEN GREAT COMPANIES FAIL, THEY'RE GONE FOR-ever. When great people fail, they learn from their experience and go on to pursue new ventures with a greater chance of success. Value the journey just as much as the destination.

HOW TO REACH

YOUR
DESTINATION

How to Reach Your Destination.

Noah Glass
Founder and CEO, OLO

JUST AFTER LAUNCHING MY FIRST VENTURE-BACKED, entrepreneurial endeavor, I had the great fortune of breaking bread with one of my dot com startup heroes. He was a brash, to-the-point kind of guy, and he left me with a nugget of advice that has stuck with me and guided me over the past seven years of high highs and low lows:

"Every little assumption in your business model is wrong. Some are slightly wrong. Some are totally wrong. It's your job to question every assumption and course correct along the way to reach your destination."

It was hard-earned knowledge, and it has served me well over the years. OLO's goal—our destination—is the same today as it was when I first sketched out a business plan. But the path for getting to where we are now—and the path forward from here—have been radically unlike what I had envisioned. I have found it 100% accurate that every little assumption in my business model was wrong— fortunately, many of the large assumptions were only slightly wrong.

The willingness to pause and re-evaluate uninformed early assumptions, the process of iterating to find a new assumption to test, and the perseverance to keep moving forward toward the destination have been critical to OLO's success.

A Team of One.

Scott Kaylie
Founder and CEO, QuantRunner Software

REALIZE THAT EITHER YOU (OR YOUR SMALL TEAM) are doing everything it takes to run a business, well beyond just chasing the shiny vision you have. In addition to product development and sales, you are general counsel, the head of human resources, head of administrative services, head of finance, etc. If you're not doing it, it's not getting done.

While it is unique and valuable training for how companies work in all functions (very helpful for the >99% likelihood that you will be returning to the corporate world), there are at times a grueling number of distractions that are tangential at best to the core mission of why you set out on your own to begin with.

keep trying

Keep Trying.

Al Zuckerman
Founder, Writers House

I GOT MY FIRST YALE DEGREE IN 1961. AFTER NUMER-ous failures and firings, I didn't start this business until 1974. Thirteen years of missteps. So that's my advice: keep trying.

Most definitely, starting a business is the best way to go, especially if it's in the field you love. And as you move forward, love your clients and colleagues along the way. All of it will keep you learning and making exciting discoveries.

"No" Doesn't Mean "No"—It Just Means "Not Right Now!"

Jennifer Carter Fleiss
President and Co-Founder, Rent the Runway

A BIG PART OF BEING AN ENTREPRENEUR IS BECOM-ing comfortable with hearing the word "no" and having the passion for your concept and creativity to adapt your idea to overcome any issues. A key lesson I learned while establishing Rent the Runway with my co-founder, Jennifer Hyman, is the importance of selling your concept with confidence despite the potential for naysayers. Starting a new business, you are guaranteed to be faced with skeptics, even full-out opponents, of your concept. After all, if your idea were perfect in everyone's eyes, it would most likely already exist, and any competitive advantage or barrier to entry you introduced would not be as great! As an entrepreneur, no matter if you are introducing your concept or continuing to build your company, you should constantly be selling—selling to consumers, vendors, current and potential em-ployees, investors, advisors, board members, business partners, and even yourself.

The truth is, in addition to being comfortable with hearing the word "no," an entrepreneur must know how to persevere. My co-founder's background in sales was immensely helpful in our early days, driving home the importance of approaching each interaction as a sales effort in which you had to know your audience, frame your pitch accordingly, and most importantly, never accept "no" for an answer. Instead of being discouraged by non-believers, it is the entrepreneur's job to engage his or her passion for the concept and creatively adapt it to overcome any hurdles. I recommend taking each interaction with skeptics as a learning experience about how to pivot your idea, or even to simply change the way you are framing your concept when selling it to others. When done correctly, "no" doesn't mean "no"; it just means "not right now."

For example, when we first pitched the concept of Rent the Runway to potential designer partners, they expressed concern that renting dresses for 15% of the retail price would cannibalize their business and negatively impact their brands. For my co-founder and me, hearing this type of feedback from someone like Diane von Furstenberg—CFDA president, connected designer, and long-time role model of ours—was initially disheartening. Pitching our concept to our dream designer partners, only to find that these supplier relationships were unstable, was initially disheartening. At that point, we had to regroup, sell ourselves on the idea that our business would persevere, and re-envision the way we approached our relationships with designers. We had to stay motivated and maintain our stamina to rethink, tweak, and keep testing our concept.

How could we convince skeptics that Rent the Runway would not take business away from top designers? More importantly, how could we convince them that it would actually *benefit* these designers? Our answer was to reframe Rent the Runway as an experiential brand marketing channel for designers. After all, Rent the Runway would offer its target customer, who is younger than that of the designer brands we encountered, the chance to experience the glamour of designer products at a more accessible price point, to build a memory with that brand, and to thereby be more inclined to purchase the brand's products later in life.

In the end, it was not just reframing, but also perseverance, that finally resulted in Rent the Runway's success. We went back to Diane von Furstenberg again and again ... and again, as we did with hundreds of other designer brands. It often took as many as ten meetings and a substantial amount of patience to allow designers to work at their own pace and become comfortable with our product until they committed to selling their pieces to us. Today, Rent the Runway has over 170 designer partners with whom we continue to maintain the strongest of relationships. Most importantly, however, we have been able to grow the company because, as founders, we continued to believe in and evolve our company despite thousands of "nos."

There are lots of ups and downs in entrepreneurship, as not everyone will love your idea, but each negative response is an opportunity to learn and adapt. A great partner and a supportive team can also be helpful in getting through what are sure to be some challenging times.

Don't Give Up.

Linda Tong
Chief Product Officer, Tapjoy

WORK ON AN IDEA YOU BELIEVE IN WITH ALL YOUR heart and soul. You're going to have days that suck. You're going to question yourself. Others will question you, your idea, your approach, everything.

When push comes to shove, you're going to wonder whether you should quit, and when that time comes, you'll need to dig deep and remember why you're doing what you're doing. Have confidence and believe in yourself and your idea. This happens to everyone, and the winners are the entrepreneurs who keep going when hope seems lost.

Unplug.

Pete Land
Partner and Co-Founder, Tamarack Media

WHEN YOU START YOUR OWN BUSINESS, YOU DIS-solve the barrier between your personal and professional lives. You feel ultimately responsible for everything that happens with your business, so even when you're not "at work," you will compulsively check your messages. And then you will compulsively respond to every single one of those messages. Your responsiveness will earn you a reputation of being reliable and trustworthy. It will also threaten your relationships, your health, and your sanity.

You must unplug from work. Turn off your smartphone when you're out at dinner. Designate a room in your home where technology is off limits. Go to the wilderness for two weeks every summer. Take a month off to travel with your partner.

Unplugged time will not only improve your personal life—it will give you space to contemplate the big-picture questions facing your work. It will give you fuel to sustain your workaholic lifestyle. And it will give you more ways to connect with your colleagues, clients, and customers.

The Chicken Itch.

Marc Cenedella
Founder, TheLadders

YOU'VE AWOKEN FROM A DREAM. IT ALL SEEMED SO real—the joy, the success, the elation of accomplishment. They've strewn your name in ribbons across the sky, carved multi-colored tattoos in your image, renamed August in your honor, soothed infants by cooing your name.

It all seemed so real. So very, very real.

You saw a different future: the future as it might be, the future that only you can create. A future that hides in the harnesses of your head, shines like bright sun reflected on glass, peeks from behind your pupils. It is the future dream that encompasses everything you ever wanted to do, everything that is inside of you, and everything that you will ever be.

And it was beautiful.

You also dreamed of fear: fear like a serpent clutching your spine, twisting at an emptiness inside of you; the blood gurgling in your ears, every pulse a footfall closer to your demise; a fear that doesn't so much make it impossible to open your eyes as suck them shut from the inside.

Everything you ever had—and you've gone and wasted it all. Spent it on a spam hallucination of grandeur; lost it to the false joker god of ambition; pissed it away on a totem purchase of pride.

You were tiny, alone, and afraid.

And you loved it.

You know now that the dream requires the fear; that the victory is composed of defeats; that the redemption in fact *comes from* the failure. You know that the dream is beautiful and you want it more than anything that has ever been born or bred or believed inside of you.

You are an entrepreneur.

In my East Asian trading days, I learned a saying: "In Japan, everybody wants to be the tail of the dragon; in Taiwan, everybody wants to be the head of the chicken." It's one of the few cross-cultural comparisons I've ever heard quoted by both sides approvingly, with an air of smug superiority.

So there's something inside of you that wants to be the head of the chicken. You'd probably like to make it a big huge chicken. (Did you know that chickens are actually dinosaurs that made it through the Extinction? Find your niche, baby!)

That's good—poultry ambition is good. You're going to need it.

As for me, I, too, had the chicken itch.

I'd joined HotJobs.com in April 2000 and helped sell the company to Yahoo! in February 2002 for $436 million. And Yahoo!, being three thousand employees at the time, was too large a dragon for me.

So I tried, and failed, at ventures ... nothing ventured with nothing gained from them.

I tried to raise money to buy Dice.com, I consulted and tried to raise money for an hourly job board startup (damn clever idea—apply by phone!). I tried to find a way, an angle, into any of the Internet, or recruitment, or Internet recruitment businesses that I found fascinating, compelling, haunting.

I didn't plan to go two years without a paycheck, to find myself cashing my last unemployment check, to be feeding myself by day-trading options (month-trading, really, but that's another story), to have ice cubes of fear scratching like keys on a car door through my veins as I set out for my business school's fifth reunion unemployed, unpaid, undone.

I didn't plan to ... but there I was.

And I guess the advice I have for dreamers is that regardless of your situation, if you intend to dream, there is one thing you must invest in. Guinness. (Or Venti Lattes, or green tea, or whatever your social drink just so happens to be.) I was fortunate enough to have met three of the best dreamers I've met in my life at HotJobs, and talking about dreaming with them over Guinness was the heady stuff that keeps you believing that it is not a setting sun—it's just rising someplace else in the world right now, and your turn is coming.

And, eventually, after a series of bad ideas, after a progression of failures, after watching the marketplace while it slept, and guessing, guessing at what it meant, I hit upon a good idea. Perhaps a great one. Perhaps something that could help the customers who didn't know they needed it yet. Maybe something that could change the world.

I was alive, incandescent, glowing.

And I was incompetent at everything I needed to be successful.

But I wasn't going to be stopped.

I bought FrontPage from Microsoft, *Dreamweaver for Dummies*, and a slice of a shared server in Jersey; anything, anything, so I could try to get "it" live: a site, a demo ... hell, even brochureware would've been a good start.

But it was useless and impossible. FrontPage wouldn't make any pages, front or back, Dreamweaver didn't, and a slice of Jersey isn't enough to build a business on unless you're a reality TV show. I grew frustrated. This stuff wasn't designed to help entrepreneurs like me get off the ground. It was window dressing. It was candy. It was fluff.

So I went out and talked to a bunch of developers.

I told them about the dream, I told them about the future, I told them about the celebrations and songs and victories and beauty that were just over the hill. I told them everything—truthfully, urgently, desperately.

But they didn't understand the dream. They thought about it for a few days and came back to tell me it would take three months and $30,000 to build a prototype.

And I didn't want to wait, and I didn't want to pay, and I didn't know how the dream was going to be helped by a "prototype" (which, I suspected, when loosely translated from the technical jargon meant, "Hey, it worked during the meeting!")

But the dream had burned itself to the inside of my eyeballs.

I went to the Barnes & Noble in Union Square, Manhattan, and bought the books that would teach me to dream in code. I bought the whole collection: *MySQL Cookbook, PHP Functions, MySQL* and *PHP for Dummies*, and what turned out to be my core curriculum and my saving grace: *MySQL and PHP for Web Development* (you can't hear it right now, but every time I read those words, angels in heaven sing to me.)

Now let me tell you what those days and nights were like.

With a beach chair I'd bought at JazzFest, I'd prop the book on one knee and the keyboard on the other in my East Village apartment. There was no night, there was no day. I'd fall asleep reading in Tompkins Square Park, gulp down functions over soba at Sobaya, wander 3:00 a.m. streets to clear my head, and go back for more.

Need to figure out how to build an email system? That's Chapter 29! Code not doing what you need it to do? Google the text of the error message! Unsure if the public site works? Call the cousins!

Three weeks of fever, fever, fever, and I'd taught myself to code, wrought my dream from bits, and pushed the button to make the site live.

Now if you ever take a look at the site I built in those three weeks of August 2003, you will find it easy to believe that I did it all by myself. But the important thing was that it was *live*! And once something is live, it can get better.

And living is the second most important thing for your dream, your vision.

Living can only occur when all of those "early days" tasks—those discrete bits of work that need to be done so that your startup can *start*—are brought to life with nothing but your spirit and zeal and energy and Yankee ingenuity and Zen intensity and passion and desire. Nothing will conquer the tasks like you on fire.

But the *most* important thing for your dream is that it be True. That it will mean something to the customers, that it will create the future you dreamed of, that it will make the days brighter, cars faster, TVs bigger, friendships better, abs tighter, and games more addictive.

That it will change the world.

If your dream is a good one, if you've done the night-watching of the marketplace, if you've listened correctly, if you have destiny, if you've earned your place at the customer's table, then the heaven-singing angels and the check-signing angels will be your boon companions.

And you will find your way through.

If ... your dream is a good one and to it you remain True.

FROM EXPERIENCE.

RIGHT MONEY

VS

WRONG MONEY

Two Pieces of Advice.

Willis "Chip" Arndt, Jr.
Managing Partner, A R N D T Strategies, LTD

1ST PIECE OF ADVICE:
"SMALL WINS LEAD TO LARGE WINS"

One of the best pieces of advice I received, after I became an entrepreneur and started my own businesses from scratch, came from a close friend in advertising sales at the then fledgling *New York Times* online edition. He simply said, "Small wins early, one at a time, always lead to the quickest path to profitability and bigger wins later." What he meant by this was that people starting a business often think that everyone else will get their vision and buy into it overnight, which, of course, will lead to landing large clients immediately who either want to buy your product(s) or close a major strategic partnership. This strategy then gives you credibility in the marketplace and the seeming quickest path to profitability. However, 99% of the time, this is not the case.

Large companies and/or major clients have other priorities and many decision makers to get on board before they will work with you. Large wins come most often after the marketplace sees traction. Always approach the large companies and go after the gold ring, but parallel process this business development and sales effort with signing up small clients and strategic partners. And, thus, each time you go back to the larger client or partner to get them on board, you can show progress and buy-in from the marketplace, which equates to them taking a more serious look at what they are missing. I guess this could all be boiled down to one sentence: Think big and create small wins along the way to reach profitability quickly, because as soon as you are profitable, everyone will look at your company.

2ND PIECE OF ADVICE:
"RIGHT MONEY VS. WRONG MONEY"

Don't ever take just any investor's money. As an entrepreneur, the hardest part of starting a venture is most often getting money in the door to open your business. Because of this, entrepreneurs often take whoever money they can bring in quickly. This is a huge mistake.

You want to ensure that you bring in the "right" money from people you trust and who believe in the long-term path to building a viable company with you. Too many times, entrepreneurs bring in the "wrong" money, which leads to turmoil (investor pressure, misunderstandings, lawsuits, and a great amount of time dealing with investor expectations) down the road when things are not going well, and often the demise of the company.

My rule of thumb is simple. If, in your gut, you neither like the people nor trust the people who are offering you money, then move on. There is always money available to invest in good ideas. It may take you a bit longer to find the "right" money, but only bring in investor money from people who have a good track record and those whom you trust will trust you. Every startup will experience bumps in the road and unforeseen issues, so you want investors aboard who are patient, understand who you are, and are NOT investing in you to make a quick buck! Building a business takes time, and you should spend just as much time finding the right investors as you do the right management team!

Ten Things I Wish I Had Known Before Founding a Company.

Kate L. Harrison
Founder and CEO, Green Life Guides, LLC

YOU AND I ARE PROBABLY NOT THAT SIMILAR. IF YOU are reading this book, it is likely that you want to be an entrepreneur. I did not.

My company grew out of a book I wrote while in graduate school on how to plan a green wedding. To keep the book up to date, I started a blog, which morphed into a website. When I saw that the site was building a following, I enrolled in the Entrepreneurial Business Planning Course at the School of Management to learn more about the market and how my site fit into the wedding industry landscape. When the business plan my team created won two business plan competitions, and I was accepted into the Yale Entrepreneurial Institute's Summer Fellows program, I found the courage to leave the environmental policy career path I was on to give running a startup a try. There was only one problem: my business plan called for over $1 million, and it was the summer of 2009—the middle of the Great Recession. That, and I had no idea what I was doing.

Over the last three years, I have raised the initial funds I needed and more—and have grown my site into the leading green brand in the wedding industry. However, this endeavor has not gone as I planned at all, and each year has brought unique opportunities and challenges. The learning curve has been steep, I have made a hundred mistakes, and the future is unclear. One thing is certain: I am having the time of my life!

Looking back, there are a number of lessons that stand out, which I believe might be helpful for others to hear. So, without further ado, here are the ten things I wish I had known before I started my company.

#1 IT WILL TAKE LONGER AND COST MORE, EVEN AFTER YOU ACCOUNT FOR IT TAKING LONGER AND COSTING MORE.

When my professors told me I needed to raise over $1 million to start my company, I literally laughed out loud. It was a sum so large I could not imagine spending it, let alone asking for it; yet three years later, I have raised more than that—and it is still not enough! Everything costs more and takes longer than you can possibly imagine. Sometimes it feels like the rest of the world is moving through molasses because even if you work with amazing people who estimate accurately, deliver reliably (aka *unicorns*), there are unforeseen technical challenges and the inevitable project "scope creep" to contend with. As one advisor told me, "To be accurate in your projections, you need to double your cost and add a zero to your time estimate. Leave room for error, and make sure your investors are prepared to put in additional capital."

#2 BEING A CEO IS 50% RAISING MONEY, 40% ADMINISTRATION AND PROJECT MANAGEMENT, 5% PARTNERSHIPS, AND 5% PROJECTS YOU SHOULD HAND OFF BUT CAN'T HELP WORKING ON.

I love writing. I love making deals. I love working out new systems. I love design and marketing and user experience. Sadly, none of these are directly my job anymore. I am a CEO. That means setting the vision, funding the vision, and helping my employees execute the vision. I have heard people compare being a CEO to being a parent—and as a mother of both a son and a company, I think this is true. Both are acts of devotion and love, and both require a great deal of personal sacrifice. You have to care more about the long-term result than the day-to-day to be able to keep your eye on the prize and keep moving forward when times get tough. It is hard to let go of the day-to-day pieces of running the company and move from doing them to overseeing them, but if you don't succeed in delegating, your company will never be bigger than you are. The takeaway is: find people you trust, train them well, and then get out of their way.

#3 IF YOU BUILD IT, THEY WON'T NECESSARILY COME.

Creating a cool product or website is rarely enough to bring success, as viral growth is not a reality for most companies. You should assume yours will require a lot of help to get where it needs to go and will take lots of time and money (see #1). You need a very strong marketing plan, and, ideally, a great co-founder, CMO, or world-class firm to help you along the way. Your business plan won't ever just execute itself. It is crucial to make sure that every sign of growth in your model is tied to a marketing action item in real life.

#4 TRAFFIC DOES NOT EQUAL SALES.

Do not assume that just because more and more people come to your site they will buy what you are selling at the same rate. There are different types of traffic, and the key to monetizing is attracting the right kind of traffic.

#5 TRAFFIC DOES NOT EQUAL ADVERTISING DOLLARS.

I run one of the most targeted and premium sites in the country that attracts wealthy women, ages twenty-five to thirty-five, with a green leaning—right before the biggest purchase of their young adult lives—yet selling ads against our traffic has been extremely difficult. In order to attract national advertisers, you need to have hundreds of thousands of visitors each month. Even then, the CPM (cost per thousand) views you can fetch will be relatively small. Because of the explosive growth of the number of online sites, and the relative stagnation of ad dollars being spent online, I would recommend keeping impression-based ad sales out of your model entirely, if possible. Let it be an upside if you can make it work at all.

#6 BUYING LISTS RARELY WORKS.

At first, it sounds like an easy way to expand your business efficiently, but most list-selling companies are borderline unethical, and most recipients on the lists they are selling do not want to hear from you. There a lot of techniques you can use to help build up a legitimate list of interested or potential clients. Explore those instead. There are marketing companies that focus on list-building that may also help you grow this aspect of your business.

#7 DO ONE THING WELL BEFORE EXPANDING.

Entrepreneurs are creative, energetic, and like to say *yes*. We also are big dreamers. The hardest thing to do as an entrepreneur is to say no or to put things off for later when we want to do them now. When I started Green Bride Guide, I had a clear vision: ideas, products, and services coming together in a unique space. I started building all three at once, and it diluted the effectiveness of each of them. Pick your first product or your first market carefully, and don't allow yourself to move forward until you have nailed it.

#8 THINK ABOUT WHAT RUNNING THE BUSINESS WILL MEAN ON A DAY-TO-DAY BASIS BEFORE YOU START.

Every company has different challenges and different needs. A content site means writers, a distribution network, and ad reps. A shopping site means warehousing, customer service, and returns. A drop-ship site means managing remote vendors, outdated stocking information, and customer confusion. A directory site means lots of sales reps, a sophisticated customer relationship management (CRM) system, recurring billing, and customer service people dedicated to helping vendors build their profiles. Manufacturing is its own can of worms. When you think about your company, think about the type of challenges you might face and ask if they are things you personally want to deal with. If yes, make sure you have a clear plan to overcome them and speak to other people in similar situations about their challenges and their solutions.

#9 FIND A WAY TO BENCHMARK AND MEASURE EVERYTHING.

In order to know whether something works and to measure your return on investment (ROI), you must have reliable data. Whether you hand out a postcard at a tradeshow or run an advertisement on a partner site, invest the time and money in tracking the results. The more you know about actual results, the more efficient you will become.

#10 TAKE TIME AWAY FROM YOUR COMPANY ONCE EACH QUARTER.

Working as many hours as you do (or soon will), it is very hard to see the big picture. Giving your mind time to breathe every few months can be pivotal to your progress. There is no such thing as a real vacation when you are an entrepreneur—I've found that it is impossible to really shut it off—but taking scheduled time away from your team to think, whether on a mountaintop with your family or in another room by yourself, makes a big difference. Stepping back will reveal the most obvious truths about what you are doing and save you time and money in the long run.

Four Lessons They Don't Teach in Business School
(Even at the Yale School of Management!)

Seth Goldman
Co-Founder and TeaEO, Honest Tea, Inc.

I ALWAYS IMAGINED I'D END UP IN LAW SCHOOL AND then go into politics (and I'm pretty sure my mother felt the same way). But I've found that business can be just as powerful a vehicle for changing our society, and perhaps a little more creative. (Not to mention, thirst-quenching.)

I learned a great deal during my two years at the Yale School of Management that helped make me a more effective TeaEO. While I'd like to think I arrived in New Haven with some marketing savvy and awareness of how to manage teams, at SOM I gained fluency in financial statements and strategy that helped make me more credible to investors, who also gained confidence from seeing the degree. And, of course, Yale is where I met my co-founder, Barry Nalebuff, who was my professor at the time, and has been an invaluable partner ever since.

But there were four key lessons not covered in SOM courses that I learned the hard way as an entrepreneur:

#1 SALES ARE JOB ONE.

Sometimes business schools undervalue the importance of selling because it's not perceived as an "MBA-skill." While business schools spend hours on marketing positioning charts and cash flow spreadsheets, they often overlook the very basic but essential tools of how to close a sale. If Honest Tea were to design an MBA course in sales, it might include topics like:

⇨ Getting the appointment: the fine art of stalking/harassment/persistence.

⇨ Are the drinks cold? How to make sure every detail is covered.

⇨ Bonding with your client: which sport does the buyer's daughter play?

⇨ Green and healthier are good: for your business and your wallet.

#2 PEOPLE WILL STEAL.

I guess I was naïve, but I thought it was safe to assume that when we sold tea to someone, they would pay us for it. In our early years, we were cheated by shadowy distributors who told us how excited they were to be our partners, then took our cases and disappeared. We never lost enough money to make it worth suing someone, but we came close a few times, and when you're just getting started, every dollar counts.

⇨ Lesson: make sure new customers pay at least half of their order up front, or run a credit check. Ship smaller orders in the beginning, even if it makes your freight costs less efficient.

#3 SPREADSHEETS LIE.

Well, they don't actually lie, but business schools put so much emphasis on sales projections and assumptions that an MBA entrepreneur actually starts to believe them. If you're spending too much time behind the laptop, it means you're short one salesman! Spreadsheets also fail to take into account all the sweat and effort it takes to sell a case, as well as the unpleasant surprises that inevitably happen, such as the customer who doesn't pay (see lesson two), the railroad car full of tea that gets frozen in North Dakota, the broken boiler at the bottling plant, the upside down labels ... you get the idea.

⇨ Lesson: Once you've developed your annual projection, cut your sales by 40% and raise your expenses by 50%, and make sure you've got the cash to weather that scenario.

#4 BUSINESS CAN BE A LOT MORE FUN, INSPIRING, AND POWERFUL THAN BUSINESS SCHOOL SUGGESTS.

There's a tendency in the classroom to be overly analytical and reserved. At Honest Tea we love creating new products that surprise and delight people. We love spreading the word about our tea in new and novel ways, and we are proud that we've been able to expand an idea that started at my kitchen counter to more than 100,000 store shelves across the country. Finally, we're excited to help lead a new generation of mission-focused businesses that seek to address social and environmental issues as they grow. Our political leaders haven't shown much daring in their task of improving the world, but today's rising generation of social and business entrepreneurs are just getting started.

Optimize.

Dan Friedman
Co-Founder and President, Thinkful

HERE'S THE ADVICE I WAS GIVEN THAT PROVED MOST true for me: Figure out whether you care more about whom you work with or what you work on. Optimize for one, and the rest will follow.

273

YOU ARE ∞ ALWAYS A SHOESHINER

You Are Always a Shoeshiner.

Lee Mergy
Senior Managing Director and Co-Founder, Galt & Company

IN 2003, I, ALONG WITH TWO OTHER PARTNERS, LEFT an established company to start a new firm, Galt & Company. Galt & Company is now a leading strategy and organizational consulting firm that helps well-managed companies deliver and sustain superior shareholder returns. But at the time we started the company, we had nothing more than our individual reputations upon which to build the business.

One of the best pieces of advice I received when thinking through how to structure and build the company was to "always think of yourself as a shoeshiner." What that meant was thinking about the business much like a shoeshiner might think of his/her business:

⇨ Stay humble and customer-focused. No matter what business you are in, you are serving your customers. You differentiate yourself by how well you satisfy, and keep satisfying, your customers' needs. Don't become so enamored with your idea or product that you believe it will "sell itself." There is always a better widget waiting in the wings.

What will make your ideas successful is your personal ability to convince customers that you stand behind what you are selling.

⇨ Stock up on your emotional capital. Prior to starting our business, my partners and I spent a lot of time calculating our expenses and financial burn rate before we thought we would become profitable. However, when starting a business, the real burn rate is emotional. Be prepared for disappointments and emotional letdowns, and make sure you have partners who are emotionally prepared for the uncertainties associated with any startup.

⇨ Focus only on the critical requirements. Many startup companies get distracted by the trappings of a new business. Focus only on those aspects of the business that are critical to delivering your product to the customer. Too often, businesses over-invest in buildings, infrastructure, and networks "in advance" of business materializing—really in "hope" that something will fill the pipeline they have built. As a result, the business is never able to recover from the initial investment. Think of the many hundreds of millions of dollars solar energy firm Solyndra spent building an edifice for their company in anticipation of the huge future demand for solar products, only to drive quickly into bankruptcy.

⇨ The value of controlling your own destiny. One of the greatest pieces of advice we received early on came from a private equity advisor who had invested in many startup companies. He kept telling us that we both underestimated the differentiation of our offer and the upside associated with controlling our own destiny. In hindsight, his encouragement was invaluable. By controlling which customers we serve and how we serve those customers, we have been able to generate superior results for them and establish a brand reputation that far exceeds that of our prior firm. Having the courage to work for yourself, not others, and thus control your own destiny, provides emotional and financial benefits that cannot be overstated.

I maintain this mindset today as my partners and I enter our tenth year of business together at Galt & Company. The firm has grown steadily over that decade, even in today's challenging economic environment, because we constantly ensure we are focused on these key components of the advice received when we first started the business.

you don't NEED A Hoodie

Three Things I Wish I'd Learned Earlier.

Linda Rottenberg
Co-Founder & CEO, Endeavor
Author, *Crazy Is a Compliment:
The Power of Zigging When Everyone Else Zags*

FIRST, YOU DON'T NEED A HOODIE TO BE AN ENTRE-preneur. We live in a time of uncertainty. Our companies and our jobs are no longer secure. To survive, we all need to continually re-invent ourselves. Whether you work at a large corporation, a non-profit, or a mom-and-pop, you need to be nimble, adaptive, and daring—and maybe even a little crazy. Everyone needs to think and act like an entrepreneur.

Two decades ago, the word "entrepreneur" was not very popular. Most people viewed it as this rarefied term that applied only to the fastest-growing companies led mainly by young male techies who lived in Silicon Valley and dressed in hoodies.

Now entrepreneurship is everywhere. And it doesn't just mean starting a company. It means undertaking any bold venture—from selling crafts out of your basement to starting a nonprofit to propos-ing a new initiative in your corporation. The techniques involved in sharpening your idea, facing down critics, recruiting boosters, and handling setbacks apply in every realm of work. You don't need a hoodie to be an entrepreneur!

Second, crazy is a compliment. You can't rock the boat without being told you're off your rocker. That goes for those who start companies—Henry Ford was called "Crazy Henry"; Walmart was "just another of Sam's crazy ideas." But it also goes for those starting initiatives inside existing companies, like leaders at Clorox, AT&T, and ESPN.

I, too, was called crazy twenty years ago, so I made it my motto. *Crazy is a compliment. And if you're not called crazy, that means you're not thinking big enough.* After two decades supporting thousands of entrepreneurs around the world, I've learned this: You have to give yourself permission to be contrarian, to stop planning and start doing—to zig when everyone else zags.

Third, don't bet the farm. One of the trickiest questions for anyone who dreams of starting something new—whether a company, a neighborhood initiative, or an innovation at work—is how far should you go? Convention says: Go all in. Sell the baseball card collection. Mortgage the house. Bet the farm. McDonald's founder, Ray Kroc, captured this sentiment. "If you're not a risk taker, you should get the hell out of business." Like a lot of the lore around business, this myth appeals to a kind of macho bravado. The phrase "bet the farm" comes from poker tables in the Wild West.

Well, boys will be boys, but entrepreneurs will be savvy. The vast majority of the 1,000 entrepreneurs I've mentored are not risk maximizers. They are risk minimizers.

Entrepreneurship at its core is a continuous balancing act between taking risk and reducing risk. Dream makers need to do both.

Hard-Won Lessons from the Bottom of Silicon Valley.

Scott Faber
Founder, Ingenio.com

I AM THE FOUNDER OF A COMPANY CALLED ETHER. com, which became Keen.com, and eventually Ingenio.com. I started the company in April 1999, when the Internet bubble economy was at its frothiest. In a matter of months, the company I had contemplated alone in my pajamas was suddenly worth half a billion dollars. Over the ensuing decade, we experienced a roller coaster ride of boom and bust, heartbreak and euphoria, and everything in between. Here are some lessons I learned along the way:

LESSON #1: ZERO TO ONE IS THE HARDEST PART.

If you're having a hard time getting your startup off the ground, don't despair. The good news is that getting from zero to one is the hardest part. In the beginning, you have nothing—no co-founder, no employees, no customers, no money. You try to get someone to join your company, but there's nothing to join! It's just you and your idea and passion, like an astronaut floating in space with nothing to push off from.

Well, this is why founders make the big bucks in the end. If you can get through this, you can get through anything. Later you'll have to achieve business-development deals and financings and product milestones, and while those all sound difficult, by then you'll have a whole team and momentum—a whole spaceship you can steer. If you're at the beginning, nothing is as difficult as what you're doing right now. So take solace in that, and continue full speed ahead!

LESSON #2: AVOID THE PHYSICAL WORLD IF YOU CAN.

The rise of the digital age is a one-time event. In the past, the older generation most always had a leg up on the young in business. But this is one of the few times when that is no longer true. You, the young, are uniquely suited to take advantage of the new age. You live digitally better than we do—you Tweet, you check in on FourSquare, you make friends using Highlight—and so are uniquely suited to start and manage digital companies.

At forty-two, I'm already over the hill. I'm on Facebook, but I don't Tweet. I'm not the mayor of the corner Starbucks on Four-Square. In digital businesses, it's the one time when investors are favoring the twenty-five-year-old CEO over the forty-five-year-old. I've got a VC friend who invests in digital businesses and says, "No founders over forty allowed in my office." So, with all these advantages in your favor, it makes sense to avoid the physical world if you can and do a pure-digital play. It's also much easier and faster. To borrow a phrase from Nicholas Negroponte, "Try and work with bits, not atoms."

LESSON #3: TAKE SOME COMPUTER SCIENCE NOW.

At Yale I studied English and then as a second major, mechanical engineering, which ended up not being very useful. I wish I had taken more computer science. Here at school, you don't realize how good you have it. It's a thousand times easier to learn a bit of computer science now than later. And the reason for that is that computer science requires attention to detail—if one comma is out of place, the whole algorithm won't work. When you're thirty years old trying to learn that stuff, you might spend three days hung up on that one comma. Whereas in a dorm, the guy next to you leans over to your screen and says, "Oh, you've got to add a comma there." You learn by osmosis. And while it might seem like it'll last forever, trust me you won't find this fertile learning environment again.

LESSON #4: GET A CO-FOUNDER WHOSE SKILLSET IS COMPLEMENTARY TO YOURS.

Ever notice that the great entrepreneurs like Steve Jobs and Bill Gates tend to have a bearded co-founder with a different skillset? It's the Steve Wozniaks, the Paul Allens, who provide the technical wizardly alongside the visionaries. Bearded or not, it's essential to have a co-founder whose skillset fills in everything you're not so good at. In the technology space, it helps to have at least one founder be technical. Otherwise, you're at the whim of engineers and consultants. Don't be afraid to share your equity with such a co-founder.

LESSON #5: I'D RATHER HAVE A SLICE OF WATERMELON THAN A WHOLE RAISIN.

A lot of fighting can go into in divvying up founder stakes, but it's not worth blowing up over. Startup success is often binary: companies tend to either be worth a whole lot, or zero. So aim for success in the big picture, not the rounding errors. If you're too tightfisted with your equity, you might stay on your own, and your company may never grow beyond a mere raisin. But if it's successful, it'll be big like a watermelon, and there'll be hearty slices for everyone. So while of course you want to maximize your own share, be fair, even if feels like you're cutting into your share. It's rare that a company is worth only a few hundred thousand dollars, and whoever got twenty-eight percent is happy and whoever got eighteen percent is unhappy.

LESSON #6: YOUR TRAIN MUST BE LEAVING.

When you're dealing with investors, it's not good if any one of them feels like you're absolutely beholden to them in order to move forward. If they sense this, they'll drag you out for months and find ways to rationalize your valuation down to nothing. After all, early-stage startups are mainly ideas, so anyone can make the case for them to be worth any value from many millions of dollars down to zero. To avoid this, make sure your train is leaving with or without them.

Let's say you have ten angel investors, all of whom you can tell are interested, but no one's willing to make the first big leap on board. You need to generate your own momentum. Announce that you are self-financing, at a certain valuation and certain terms, but that you're willing to make space for angel investors (choose reasonable numbers). If self-financing is not at all an option, choose friends or family or the friendliest angel. Once your train is leaving, you'll be surprised how many investors hop aboard—to the point where you may no longer have to contribute any money yourself. The leaving train draws upon an odd facet of the investor mind: they're often motivated more by the *fear* of missing out on the next big thing than by the *desire* for the upside of your deal. A leaving train triggers both of these: the desire to move forward and the fear of getting left behind.

LESSON #7: ANGELS ARE GREAT; 1,000 ANGELS ARE EVEN BETTER.

The great thing about angel investors is that they tend to ride along peacefully and easily. If there are many of them, no single one of them will wield an overly powerful stake in your company. Best of all, once angels are on board, they're on your side. Since they'll benefit from your success, they'll do anything for you: buy your product, introduce you to larger investors, spread the good word. The extreme example of this is Kickstarter. Having backing from the Kickstarter community is like having 1,000 angels. A friend of mine raised a lot of money to launch a mobile app, however, his app was trounced by one from another company that had raised a tenth of what he had, but had done so through 1,000 angels on Kickstarter. Those thousand angels became the customers and evangelists that provided the all-important critical mass early on. Any future project I do, I'll do through Kickstarter, even if I don't need the money.

LESSON #8: TELL A STORY AND DEMO EARLY.

When pitching venture capitalists, some entrepreneurs start in with their PowerPoint deck and drone through the slides bullet by bullet. This makes investors' eyes glaze over. Be sure to tell a story—one that has a compelling beginning and ends with your company being the triumphant hero. Ideally, your slides only provide accompanying information and graphics. It should be mainly about the story. Stories are how humans have been transmitting ideas for eons—investor pitches are no different. And be sure to have a hands-on demo be part of your story, ideally on the early side. Having observed lots of pitches and business-development meetings, I've noticed that the important decision-makers often snooze during the blah blah bullets, but then wake up as soon as the demo starts. Don't ever let them snooze—start right in with a compelling story accompanied by a demo early on.

LESSON #9: THERE IS NO GOOD OR BAD; THERE JUST IS.

A far-reaching professional career used to take decades, and afterwards, as an elderly person, you'd have gained all these Zen-like insights. The good thing about a startup career is that it speeds up time. In just a few years, you can experience the hundreds of ups and downs that used to take decades.

When I look back over all the ups and downs of my startup career, I notice something odd. All the ups—everything I thought was good at the time—ended up being bad. For instance, we gained an A-list investor, which at the time I thought could only be good news, but in the longer run, it turned out to be bad news because that investor ended up saddling us with a disastrous executive. Conversely, many of the downs—everything I thought was bad at the time—ended up being good. Sometimes it was seemingly bad news that led to, say, a prosperous idea. So with everything good ending up bad and everything bad ending up good, it's led me to the fortune-cookie insight that there is no good or bad; there just *is*.

Professional poker players make a good example of this—they often win the most on the hands that start the worst and lose the most on the hands that start the best, like a pair of aces. So don't be daunted by "bad" news or overly exuberant about the "good"—just take everything as it is and do your best with it.

Avoiding Pitfalls.

Frederick W. Smith
Chairman, CEO and Founder, FedEx Corporation

LOOKING BACK OVER FORTY YEARS TO THE FOUND-
ing of FedEx, I believe I would have benefitted greatly from the following pieces of advice I've picked up subsequently:

Do a better job of evaluating "good" vs. "best" solutions in order
to lower upfront expenses and allow faster speed to market;

Be mindful of emerging external developments that can unexpectedly and adversely affect your plans, and develop contingent alternative courses of action beforehand;

And maybe most important of all, as an old friend once told me,
"Remember that the secret to a happy life is a short memory!"

Had I known these things at the outset of my business career,
I would probably have avoided some pitfalls and certainly have
swerved around some potholes in the road.

The Top Ten Avoidable Mistakes of Entrepreneurs.

William H. Draper III
General Partner, Draper Richards LP
Co-Chair, Draper Richards Kaplan Foundation

OVER THE LAST FIFTY YEARS, I HAVE COME ACROSS and worked with an array of entrepreneurs from a variety of industries, and I have noticed that there are certain preventable blunders that seem to crop up repeatedly. To an extent, everybody has to reinvent the wheel and make his own mistakes, but I offer the following in the hope that at least *some* entrepreneurs will take *some* of these prescriptions to heart and maybe make their avoidable mistakes less costly.

#1 CREATING OVERLY OPTIMISTIC PROJECTIONS ABOUT MARKET SIZE AND CUSTOMER ACQUISITIONS.

My advice: Do your homework in terms of market research. Don't blur the line between the number of potential customers who *might possibly* buy your product and the number who actually will. Don't overlay an arbitrary percentage on the largest possible customer base when estimating potential market share.

In three words: *Know your customer.*

#2 UNDERSTANDING TIMELINES.

My advice: Remember the sage advice offered by Douglas Hofstadter, in a maxim he named after himself: "It always takes longer than you think, even when you take into account Hofstadter's Law." Wrap your mind around that one.

#3 TRYING TO DO EVERYTHING YOURSELF.

My advice: There are only twenty-four hours in a day, and you generally can't get by on less than seven hours of sleep—maybe six. Nor can you be an expert at everything. Surround yourself with an experienced team, all of whom are smarter than you.

#4 FAILING TO MASTER THE ELEVATOR PITCH.

My advice: Develop, practice, and memorize an accurate and concise message about your company's value proposition. Then get everybody else in the company to do the same, with *consistency* as a paramount goal.

#5 NOT DOWNSIZING WHEN NECESSARY.

My advice: Don't be afraid to cut back. You may lose a little face but not as much as you think. You'll lose a whole lot more face if you go out of business as a result of not having made timely cuts.

#6 BEING FLEXIBLE.

My advice: Deal with your changing reality. The market shifts. New competition arises. You have no choice but to be flexible enough to deal with the inevitable twists and turns.

#7 NOT DEVELOPING A CLEAR MARKETING PLAN.

My advice: It's not enough to have an amazing idea, or even an amazing product. How is the world going to find out about it? Start-ups often fail to put sufficient resources behind sales and marketing. Don't be one of them.

#8 BUILDING A BOARD THAT CONSISTS ONLY OF FRIENDS.

My advice: Go for every kind of diversity. Find people with industry knowledge, contacts, operational experience, and enough time to be helpful. Beware of out-of-towners; telephonic board attendance is not optimum.

#9 NOT TAKING ACTION IN A RECESSION.

My advice: This is a corollary to number 5. Make cuts in human resources as necessary, but also: get suppliers to reduce prices and give better service, improve efficiency, and turn up the heat on your competition.

#10 NOT KNOWING THE RIGHT WAY TO APPROACH VENTURE CAPITALISTS.

My advice: Be prepared. Read this chapter and this entire book. Be very clear about the problem that your company proposes to solve and who your customers will be. Provide detailed information about yourself and your key associates. After your first meeting, follow up, and don't be shy. After all, you will have the best product or service in the world. Right?

Passion, Persistence, and Pragmatism.

Sanjay H. Patel
CEO, Datanautix Inc.

BEING AN ENTREPRENEUR IS A CHALLENGING, EXCITing, and often arduous journey. Along the way, you will pick up lessons through the school of hard knocks that will help you prepare for future ventures. Sometimes learning these lessons the hard way could have been avoided "if only someone had told me." Here are my hard-learned lessons that I hope will help you with your entrepreneurial journey.

First and foremost, you have to be PASSIONATE about your entrepreneurial idea. When an investor is determining the viability of your business model, they have two things to go on—their experience as investors, and your ability to convince them that the model you are outlining is viable and transformational. If you don't believe in your idea with a passion that borders on fanatical, you are already down one strike.

The second characteristic of significant importance is PERSISTENCE. Once you have got the idea off the ground and you are running at 110%, you will hit multiple roadblocks and bumps along the way. The key to success will be your ability to jump back up, dust yourself off, and start running again. Persistence comes through when you have fallen and feel like you just don't have the energy to get up and run anymore—the difference between the winners and losers shows up now. If you don't stand up, you are down another strike.

And finally, PRAGMATISM is the behavior that will become the core foundation of your success. Knowing when to change course and bring a sense of reality to your venture can often become the difference between success and failure. Be prepared to change direction and not remain married to your original vision—markets change, competitors enter and leave, you become more knowledgeable. These are all appropriate triggers for shifts in direction. Knowing when to flex and change is a difficult step for founders of a company—having the courage to do so is what will differentiate you from other entrepreneurs. Do not let this be your third strike.

Words to the Wise.

Jon Carson
Co-Founder and CEO, BiddingForGood

HERE ARE THE FIVE MANTRAS I HAVE DEVELOPED over four startups (two winners, one neutral, and one in progress) that are the product of years of stumbles, learnings, and just plain old experience.

REALITY IS YOUR FRIEND.

The point here is to be realistic about the opportunity and the risks. The biggest role of the entrepreneur is to manage risk. You can only do that by being realistic and avoiding a common entrepreneurial pitfall of being wildly optimistic and misjudging the situation, the new hire, the market, etc., etc.

WHAT DO YOU HAVE TO BELIEVE?

This is a great header for a sheet of paper when looking at any new market, partnership, new product, etc. The things listed under the header are the key assumptions to the bet.

PLAN THE WORK AND WORK THE PLAN.

You need a plan, even if it is just a few key milestones and their related sub-elements that you have identified as mission critical. And, once you know where you need to go, then you need to focus on making it happen.

START WITH THE END IN MIND.

This comes from the well-known book, *7 Habits of Highly Successful People,* and it's a pretty valuable insight. If you don't know where you are going you'll never get there.

AT BEST, HIRING IS A 50/50 CRAP SHOOT.

Hiring great folks is critical to building the team, and it's not easy. Many folks put on a great interview, but the excellence ends there. Others get solid references and you wonder if you hired the same person. And, in other cases, you get a start from somebody you never expected. My best interview question is, "What would your worst reference say about you?" It's hard to give the answer to that question, "I work too hard," with a straight face. I have also found that having key candidates take an assessment test gives you more data. Lastly, back-channel references are the best. It's hard for candidates to game them.

Jump.

Damon Danielson
Capitalist

YOU THINK OF YOURSELF AS AN ENTREPRENEUR; I RE-
spect and admire that. I have been a serial entrepreneur since before
you were born, and through the good and the bad, I love what I do.
If you don't love what you do, stop now and do something else. Here
are a few things I've learned along the way that I hope will help you
on your journey.

Ironically, an important lesson I've learned is that in most situations, the people you communicate with are only going to remember
one thing that you say to them—if you're lucky. So try to create a
message that gets them to remember the thing you want them to
remember, and keep it short and sweet.

See, I should stop here ...

But there is one more idea I would like to share with you. Entrepreneurs fail. You are going to fail. You are going to fail many times,
if you're good. You are going to have two or three really painful failures. Sometimes it will be your fault, and many times it won't be. In
all cases, though, you are going to feel bad. Many of your peers and

people you thought were your friends are going to be unavailable. The first time this happens will be devastating to you.

But here's what you need to learn from that ...

Failure is completely overrated. I mean, it's just not that bad. Most people have an irrational fear for how bad failure will be, and the bad thing about that is that they then don't take enough risks. If you don't take intelligent risks that push your boundaries, you're not going to get much done in your life. So take intelligent risks that stretch your comfort level. And when you fail, lay low for a couple months, hit the waves or the gym—or whatever works for you. Then get up, start dreaming, and move forward again.

Jump.

What I've come to realize in my life is this: it turns out that even when it's bad, it's good.

So ... soak it up.

If you would like to learn more about entrepreneurial life, please read my book on surfing, *7 Laws of Surfing*. I wrote it for you.

Create.

And ... have fun doing it.

It's Not All About You.

Mitch Kapor
Founder, Lotus Development Corp.

YOU DESERVE LESS BLAME FOR YOUR FAILURES AND less credit for your successes than you might imagine. Therefore, be receptive to learning from what didn't work, and be very generous in sharing credit and the fruits of success with others.

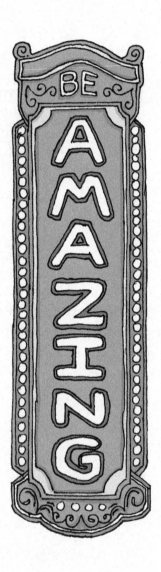

Be Amazing.

Markus Moberg
CEO and Co-Founder, Veritas Prep

GO BIG OR GO HOME? NO, GO LONG AND ENJOY IT!

Many entrepreneurs are inspired by companies like Instagram and Zappos that sold for big money, but those massive paydays are the exception, not the rule. If you really want to be an entrepreneur, do it because you enjoy creating and running a company. If all you want to do is go big, you're going to spend half your time pitching to VCs and the other half throwing Hail Marys. It will likely be eventful and fun, but you're also likely going to have to start from scratch every two to three years without building anything sustainable.

"FOLLOW YOUR DREAMS" IS MISLEADING.

You should definitely do something you're into, but if you're not amazing at it, then it should be your hobby, not your business. It's more important that you find an overlap of something you at least like fairly well with something you're naturally very good at. If you don't know what that thing is yet, travel, work some place cool, or go back to school for a couple years.

EVERY EMPLOYEE STARTS OUT ON A THREE-MONTH CONTRACT.

Tell every new employee that they will receive an evaluation after three months and that the evaluation will determine their continued employment. Show them exactly the criteria on which they will be evaluated. The right type of employee will be inspired to make a huge effort in the beginning, which then sets the framework for their attitude for a long time to come.

CONDUCT WEEKLY CHECK-INS.

Meet with each person that reports to you for thirty minutes a week and ask them what you can do for them. Ask them how they're feeling about their job. What they want to do with their career. What obstacles you can help remove. How can you make their lives easier? If your employees know you're genuinely looking out for them, they'll reciprocate. You will also avoid any pent-up frustration since you're giving them the opportunity to vent every week.

FIRE RELATIVELY QUICKLY.

A poorly performing employee is likely also an unhappy employee and that can be a cancer to your company's culture. If an employee is no longer achieving what you want or is not fitting in for whatever reason, think about the specific accomplishments or behavior you're looking for. Sit down with him and give him very specific, quantifiable goals you want him to accomplish over the next two months. If he can't meet your requirements in that two-month period, let him go. You will never regret it.

SAVE CASH.

Don't spend just because you have it. Be ready for your business to take a downturn at some point. Being an entrepreneur is about as close to pure meritocracy as you can get, yet any seasoned entrepreneur will tell you that LUCK has been a significant contributor to their success or failure. Set your company up to weather a perfect storm of bad luck someday.

PERFECTION AND TESTING WILL GRIND YOUR COMPANY TO A HALT.

Don't be so concerned about doing things the corporate way—just get the product out there and sell. Cut back on the bells and whistles, and ensure that the core of the product is solid; you'll have plenty of time to improve and add bells and whistles to your product later.

STAY AWAY FROM LAWYERS.

Someone steal your idea? Execute better than they can. Someone misrepresent your product? Overwhelm the market with positive reviews. Taking a company or person to court should be your last resort. It will pull resources and focus away from your business, and, in most cases, the only people who really win, regardless of the outcome, are the lawyers.

TRADITIONAL ADVERTISING IS FOR BRAND ESTABLISHING, AND YOU CAN'T AFFORD THAT.

Print and TV ads are great if you're Gucci or Ford, but forget about it until you have that kind of cash. Spend your money on SEO and PPC instead, or even a PR firm. Telling a great story about your business is far more effective than sharing information about your product.

THIS IS NOT A 9 TO 5 JOB.

Sometimes it's 9:00 a.m. to 5:00 p.m., sometimes it's 5:00 a.m. to 9:00 p.m. for a week or months, sometimes it's three days a week. Point is: remain flexible. Work hard when you have to, relax and enjoy your life when you're not needed. The first couple of years you have to expect all-nighters and poverty, but the sign of a well-built company is one where you can leave for a month without it crumbling.

LIVE AND DIE BY YOUR OWN OPINION.

Trust your own opinion on how your product should look and how it should work. If your taste suits that of many others, you've got yourself a business. If it doesn't, then you're not in the right industry. If you don't have a clear point of view, you're not ready to start your business. If you're trying to guess what others want or "create by committee," you'll never have a unique product or gain a competitive advantage.

IDEAS ARE WORTH THEIR WEIGHT IN GOLD. IMPLEMENTATION IS EVERYTHING.

I Wish Someone Had Told Me.

Cornelius McNab
Founder, 40Billion.com

I WISH SOMEONE HAD TOLD ME EARLIER TO JUST GO
for it, to build your dreams, and don't listen to the naysayers.

When I dreamed up 40Billion.com back in early 2008, so many
folks told me that a social funding network for startup entrepreneurs
via the Internet would never work. Just four years later, it's become a
multi-billion dollar industry, and we've worked with the government
to create new laws facilitating crowdfunding for American small
businesses to raise money and build dreams like never before.

So … build your dreams, don't listen to the naysayers, and go
for it!

Acknowledgments.

I WOULDN'T HAVE BEEN ABLE TO WRITE THIS BOOK without the assistance and generosity of many people.

First and foremost, a huge thank you to all the entrepreneurs who shared their reflections, experiences, and lessons from their own lives. You took valuable time out of your busy schedules to share insights that took you years and many difficult experiences to acquire. I hope the readers take these lessons to heart.

There are a few people from my Yale experience who were instrumental to the path I am on today, and who deserve much thanks. Bob Casey, who I first shared this book concept with in May 2012, over lunch in New Haven, for being an incredible friend, advocate for entrepreneurs, and source of infinite enthusiasm. Sean Glass, my favorite lecturer at Yale, who assigned me my first book on entrepreneurship, *Four Steps to the Epiphany,* for catalyzing modern entrepreneurship in the Yale community. David S. Rose, an outstanding boss and mentor, for your benevolence and contagious passion. This book would not have been created if it weren't for the three of you.

A number of friends, family, colleagues, and mentors listened to the dream and shared extensive feedback. Thanks for taking the time to meaningfully improve this book: Will Anderson, Ben Battaglia, Austin Bernhardt, Michael Chambers, Rosie Chambers, Don Clark Jr., Don Clark Sr., Jean Clark, David Fugate, John Gambell, Karen T. Green, Zachary Hill, Tiffany Ho, Mandy LoPresti, Taryn Miller-Stevens, Paul Miloknay, Andrew Mangino, William Oppenheimer, Agustin Paniagua, John-Michael Parker, Luke Schoenfelder, Stephanie Schwartz, Justin Stanwix, Jules Terrien, and Wendy Wolf. Thank you for all the love and support I've received from family and friends.

While I don't know any of you personally, I appreciate all of the people who have documented their experiences with the constantly evolving publishing world, whose resources help more people than you realize—especially you, Guy Kawasaki.

This book would also not have been possible without a few other people who have provided incredible industry insight and acted as cheerleaders along the way. Frederick Berg, Jr., you have been unbelievably helpful as a legal adviser and connector to other selfless individuals, and you have helped plant seeds that will do great in the world and be long-lasting. David B. Wolf, whose expertise in the publishing world made a complicated issue a breeze—thank you for taking all of my oddball questions and making sure everything was covered. Mike Smith, you have been an amazingly efficient growth hacker. Zach Harris, thank you for being the best designer I have ever worked with. Anyone looking for a talented (and incredible organized) creative, needs to check out www.birdsandkinds.com. Polly Letofsky, thank you for being a trailblazer in the modern publishing world, making this a product we can all be proud of. Donna Mazzitelli, thank you for being the editor of my dreams. I had no idea what the end product would look like, but your shepherding and enthusiasm have made this fun.

I want to end by thanking my family.

My brother, Matt, for his years of insights, feedback, and patience with every project I have ever been a part of. I owe the ultimate debt of gratitude to you, and hope that I can give you half as much as you have given to me. Thank you for being there from start to finish. We have a lot more of the world to conquer together.

My fiancée, Camille, thank you for always putting things in perspective and keeping me sane. We started dating when I had a brand new startup and only a dozen pages written in this book. I don't know how TouchPoints, this book, or I would have survived without you. I love you more than words can express.

My parents, Bonnie and Michael, thank you for teaching me most of the life lessons I needed to learn and for preparing me for the ones I've had to learn on my own. You have always encouraged me to pursue anything I was interested in. You have always believed in me and trusted me to do what is best. You have given Matt, Mandy, Camille, and me a lot to live up to. Your unceasing support and selflessness are true gifts.

About the Author.

CHRIS LOPRESTI IS THE founder of TouchPoints, a consumer data technology company that helps brands connect with their community. LoPresti is also the founder and chairman of ELIS Inc., a nonprofit focused on promoting STEM education and supporting the next generation of entrepreneurs. In addition to his work with next-gen doers at ELIS Inc., LoPresti is a member of the Thousand Network, a coach at The Future Project, a member of the NationSwell Council, and a proud Eagle Scout. He has a B.A. in political science from Yale University.

ELIS Inc. & Proceeds From *Insights.*

THIS BOOK WAS CREATED TO BRING TOGETHER A community of people to share their knowledge and pay forward the help they've received throughout their individual careers. All 101 entrepreneurs volunteered their advice and experiences in this book, and at many other times in their lives, they have offered their insights for free. They all share a common desire to support entrepreneurs of every type.

The proceeds from *INSIGHTS* will go to ELIS Inc., a registered 501c3 organization created by some of the entrepreneurs in this book. The purpose of the nonprofit is to help future entrepreneurs, leaders, and innovators gain access to resources—both mentors and money.

Your contribution, by either making a direct donation or by buying this book, will help foster the next great organizations and businesses. To learn more and support this cause, please go to InsightsTheBook.com.

Let's Stay Connected.

TO STAY CONNECTED, PLEASE BE SURE TO FIND ME online by visiting my website at InsightsTheBook.com. You can also contact me at Insights@ChrisLoPresti.com. I would love to hear from you!

And one last favor ...

If you have enjoyed *Insights: Reflections from 101 of Yale's Most Successful Entrepreneurs*, please leave a review on Amazon, Barnes & Noble and Goodreads.

Thank you!

About the Press.

MERRY DISSONANCE PRESS IS A BOOK PRODUCER/INdie publisher of works of transformation, inspiration, exploration, and illumination. MDP takes a holistic approach to bringing books into the world that make a little noise and create dissonance within the whole in order that ALL can be resolved to produce beautiful harmonies.

Merry Dissonance Press works with its authors every step of the way to craft the finest books and help promote them. Dedicated to publishing award-winning books, we strive to support talented writers and assist them to discover, claim, and refine their own distinct voice. **Merry Dissonance Press** is the place where collaboration and facilitation of our shared human experiences join together to make a difference in our world.

For more information, visit http://merrydissonancepress.com/.

CPSIA information can be obtained
at www.ICGtesting.com
Printed in the USA
BVOW03s1438130717
489195BV00003B/118/P